The Game You Can Never Win

Relationship, Volume 1

Willy Lapse Laguerre

Published by Willy Lapse Laguerre, 2024.

While every precaution has been taken in the preparation of this book, the publisher assumes no responsibility for errors or omissions, or for damages resulting from the use of the information contained herein.

THE GAME YOU CAN NEVER WIN

First edition. November 10, 2024.

Copyright © 2024 Willy Lapse Laguerre.

ISBN: 979-8224140428

Written by Willy Lapse Laguerre.

Also by Willy Lapse Laguerre

Cultural Differences
The Forbidden Love

Deception
A Hustler's Journey - Against The Shadow

Fairy Tales Story
The King of Milk Tome 1
The Child Of Shadows

Poetry
Where The Shadow Can not Reach

Relationship
The Game You Can Never Win

The Shattered Veil
The Valley Of The Masks

Thriller Horror
Station 13

DEDICATION

To those who find themselves locked in battles that can't be won—whether with themselves, with others, or with the world around them. This is for the dreamers who play anyway, find courage in impossible odds, and seek meaning even in the struggle. May you discover that some games aren't meant to be won, but to reveal who you indeed are along the way.

ACKNOWLEDGMENTS

This book could not have come to life without the unwavering support of those who, like me, have struggled with life's unsolvable puzzles and unbreakable loops. I owe my deepest gratitude to the friends, mentors, and loved ones who have stood by me as I confronted my own impossible games. Thank you for your patience, honesty, and kindness.

To my readers—thank you for picking up this book and daring to look into the shadowy corners of the mind with me. Your openness to exploring life's complexities and unresolved questions keeps me inspired. This journey may have its dark and uncertain moments, but it's those who choose to walk it who remind me that perhaps, it's not about winning or losing at all.

And finally, to those who have felt the weight of expectations, the frustration of walls that won't budge, and the beauty of persistence—this book is for you.

Chapter 1 The Illusion of Perfection

Chapter 2 The Rules Are Rigged
Chapter 3 Unpacking Myths of Success
Chapter 4 Shadows of Superficiality
Chapter 5 Breaking Free from Expectations
Chapter 6 Navigating Emotional Costs
Chapter 7 Redefining Success
Chapter 8 Authenticity Over Perfection
Chapter 9 Developing Emotional Intelligence
Chapter 10 Communication: Beyond Words
Chapter 11 Fostering Mutual Growth
Chapter 12 Defining Boundaries
Chapter 13 Encouraging Self-Awareness
Chapter 14 Embracing Uncertainty
Chapter 15 The Journey to Authentic Connection

Foreword

IN A WORLD WHERE LIFE unfolds as a sequence of decisions and every moment seems calculated for effect, the thrill of competition lures us with promises of achievement, satisfaction, and perhaps even victory. Yet, as many know and few dare to admit, not every game can be won. *The Game You Cannot Win* plunges us into a reality governed by rules that twist like smoke, where the players often find themselves at the mercy of a game rigged from the start. This is a world where winning and losing are not as clear-cut as they might appear and where the illusion of control tempts us until the end.

Our story follows an unlikely hero who, armed with determination and resilience born from hardship, enters a contest designed not for triumph but for subjugation. As they delve deeper into this world—a labyrinth of deception, betrayal, and mysterious alliances—they begin to see the threads of a system carefully crafted to keep them trapped. Each step forward unravels another layer of secrets, each relationship forged proves fragile and fleeting, and every victory turns out to be a momentary illusion. The deeper our hero plunges, the clearer it becomes: some games exist solely to demonstrate how unwinnable they are.

As readers, we are drawn into this narrative of inevitability, invited to walk the razor-thin line between hope and despair. In an atmosphere thick with tension, we question, alongside our hero, the cost of freedom and the ever-shifting meaning of success. Is victory worth pursuing when the price may be one's humanity? Are there battles better left unchallenged, or does surrender signify the most accurate loss?

We explore a paradox confronting many of us through *The Game You Cannot Win*. We pursue dreams, invest in ideals, and often chase a sense of fulfillment that seems eternally out of reach. Yet here, amidst the struggle, we find the essence of our humanity. This story speaks not only to the hero's journey within the plot but to each of us who has ever faced a challenge that felt insurmountable, to those who have grappled with the price of ambition and the desire to transcend limitations.

Welcome to a world where the game board shifts with every breath, shadows hide intent, and every triumph is tinged with a faint sense of loss. As you turn these pages, prepare to confront the uneasy truth that some games are not meant to be won. Uncertainty reigns supreme in this maze of shifting loyalties, and the cost of every move is exacted in ways no player could foresee.

The Game You Cannot Win is a journey that doesn't end with answers but questions that echo long after the final page is turned. The only certainty within these lines is uncertainty itself—an ever-present reminder that in life's most profound trials, it's often not the victory that defines us but the resilience to keep playing, the courage to face the rules, and the insight to recognize when to walk away.

Chapter 1
The Illusion of Perfection

PERFECTION IN RELATIONSHIPS is an alluring notion that captivates many. It promises a seamless, idyllic partnership devoid of conflict or disappointment—a tempting prospect for those seeking everlasting happiness. However, such aspirations often stem from external influences, notably the skewed depictions churned out by the media. As these idealized portrayals permeate our consciousness through romantic films, social media, and even advertisements, they establish unattainable benchmarks. These narratives shape perceptions by showcasing only select moments of joy and harmony while omitting the inevitable struggles, leading individuals to measure

Their relationships against a fantasy. Consequently, these distorted expectations can cause dissatisfaction and emotional turmoil when reality falls short of these impossible standards.

The chapter explores this illusion of perfection and delves into how various media forms contribute to unrealistic relationship ideals, impacting personal fulfillment and relational dynamics. The narrative will examine the role of romantic comedies, where effortlessly perfect love stories become cultural touchstones that influence societal perceptions. Additionally, it will consider how social media influencers curate snapshots of so-called perfect romances, fostering parasocial bonds that blur reality and fiction. These elements, combined with advertising's tendency to equate material success with relational contentment, create a complex web of myths around love.

Furthermore, the discussion extends to the impact of celebrity culture, where high-profile unions suggest that passion must be dramatic to be meaningful. By dissecting these themes, the chapter invites readers to challenge prevailing ideals, encouraging a shift toward embracing authentic connections marked by understanding, growth, and resilience. Through this lens, it aims to offer insights into nurturing genuine relationships amidst pervasive yet misleading societal norms.

Media's Role in Shaping Relationship Ideas In a world saturated with media, our perceptions of love and relationships are often influenced more by what we see on screens than our lived experiences. Romantic comedies, for instance, play a significant role in shaping how we think about romance. Filled with seamless relationships and picture-perfect scenarios, these films can foster the unrealistic belief that love should be effortless. The protagonists typically glide through life's ups and downs with little more than a few comedic mishaps, leading viewers to internalize these notions without seeing the more profound, often messier realities of human connections. This portrayal leads many to expect their relationships to mirror those of on-screen narratives, setting them up for disappointment when encountering real-life challenges. Love, in reality, is complex and requires hard work, communication, and compromise—elements often glossed over or romanticized in film. Johnson and Holmes (2009) highlight that movies deliver exaggerated depictions of relationships that viewers may mistakenly perceive as attainable norms. Consequently, people become disillusioned when their relationships do not match these fictional ideals. Such disparities between expectation and reality can induce dissatisfaction, nurturing feelings of inadequacy among partners who struggle to maintain an unrealistic standard of affection. Social media influencers further amplify these misconceptions. Influencers paint a distorted picture of romantic bliss by curating snapshots of idealized moments. Their posts focus on carefully chosen scenes emphasizing harmony and happiness, strategically avoiding conflict or difficulty.

Followers then consume this content, believing such perfection is common, and develop parasocial relationships with these figures, often leading to dissatisfaction with their lives. This phenomenon reinforces the idea that love and happiness depend on external validation and aesthetic conformity. Gupta et al. (Breves et al., 2024) suggest an intriguing perspective on romantic parasocial relationships, noting how followers may form intense attachments based on the perceived romantic potential of influencers. Such relationships blur the boundaries between reality and fiction, encouraging individuals to base their emotional expectations on contrived personas rather than authentic interactions.

The narrative extends into consumerism, with advertising relentlessly linking material success to relationship happiness. Advertisements frequently depict luxurious lifestyles as synonymous with fulfilling partnerships, suggesting that love can be purchased or measured through consumption. The message is clear: material possessions are integral to achieving personal and relational satisfaction. However, this association skews the true essence of emotional connection, overshadowing genuine intimacy with superficial fulfillment. Consumers, therefore, might chase financial success and indulgence, mistaking these for markers of love's depth, thereby straying from the intrinsic value found in vulnerable and honest exchanges.

Public fascination with celebrity relationships adds another layer to this convoluted understanding of love. Celebrities, with their grand gestures and tabloid-worthy romances, captivate audiences worldwide. The lavish spectacles often associated with their affections, like extravagant weddings or ostentatious displays of affection, suggest that true love must be equally dramatic. Society's attention to high-profile unions promotes the idea that passion must always be tumultuous and exhilarating. The implication is that everyday gestures of care and consistency lack the enthusiasm for meaningful bonds, steering people toward valuing spectacle over substance. In this way, many may equate love solely with intensity and abandon, missing out on the quiet joys of companionship and support.

Moreover, these diverse media channels collectively propagate the myth of "perfection" in relationships, urging individuals to conform to an unattainable model of love. The illusion of faultless unions perpetuates a cycle of unrealistic expectations, where individuals strive for ideals rooted in fantasy rather than authenticity. Each depiction—from films to social media, advertisements to celebrity culture—intertwines to create a tapestry of myths surrounding what constitutes a successful relationship.

Understanding the origins of these beliefs is crucial for deconstructing the illusions perpetuated by media. It involves recognizing the selective nature of media portrayals and questioning the stereotypes they cement within societal consciousness. By fostering awareness, individuals may begin to appreciate the diversity of real-life relationships, acknowledging that each bond is unique and valid despite its imperfections. This shift in perception encourages people to embrace their journeys, focusing on building connections resilient enough to withstand life's kaleidoscope of experiences.

Impact of Perfectionism and Comparison Culture on Relationships

The pressure to maintain impeccable relationships can be overwhelming in a world seemingly obsessed with achieving perfection. This relentless pursuit of flawlessness often results in an all-consuming focus on minor imperfections, fostering excessive scrutiny and fear of failure. The constant anxiety of not living up to ideal standards creates stress that permeates every interaction, leading to dissatisfaction. Over time, this perpetuates a cycle where partners are more concerned about potential missteps than celebrating the unique dynamics that make their relationship special.

Moreover, in today's digital age, comparison culture has become omnipresent. Social media platforms showcase carefully curated snapshots of intimate connections, presenting them as benchmarks for others to aspire to. Despite knowing these representations lack authenticity, many individuals fall into the trap of juxtaposing their relationships against these distorted realities. This habit cultivates feelings of inadequacy or jealousy, making personal connections strained and unfulfilling. Instead of fostering genuine companionship, these comparisons often lead to loneliness as individuals become disconnected from their relational truths.

The idealization of partners further compounds the issue. When one partner elevates another to unrealistic heights, it places significant pressure on both parties. Such expectations are not only demanding to meet but also set the stage for disillusionment when reality fails to align with fantasy. Disappointment breeds mistrust, eroding the very foundation of love and commitment. A relationship burdened by unmet ideals is akin to walking on fragile ice; all it takes is one misstep to plunge into chaos.

To navigate the complexities of relationships while preserving emotional well-being, differentiating between healthy and unhealthy expectations becomes crucial. Encouraging openness and adaptability allows for a mutual understanding that paves the way for growth. By acknowledging each other's imperfections and embracing them as opportunities for improvement, couples can build resilient bonds based on authenticity. Communication is central to this process, fostering an environment where partners feel safe expressing vulnerabilities without fear of judgment.

Cultivating self-compassion is essential for overcoming the detrimental effects of striving for perfection. Recognizing and accepting one's flaws enable individuals to extend the same grace to their partners. When people treat themselves kindly, they are more likely to understand that imperfections do not dictate worth. This mindset shift alleviates the relentless drive for faultlessness and encourages a healthier, more realistic perspective on relationships.

Promoting authenticity within partnerships provides a solid framework for deeper connections. Celebrating individuality rather than conforming to societal molds strengthens bonds and enhances intimacy. In a world filled with facades, being genuine with one another becomes a powerful act of rebellion against artificial standards. It fosters trust and empathy, cornerstones upon which meaningful relationships thrive.

Fostering growth through flexibility involves letting go of rigid expectations about how love should manifest itself. Embracing change as an integral part of relational development reassures partners that evolving together is ordinary and necessary. Adapting to shifting circumstances reflects resilience—a quality that fortifies relationships against external pressures. Couples who navigate life's uncertainties hand in hand emerge more robust and united through shared experiences.

Concluding Thoughts

This chapter has delved into the pervasive influence of media on our perceptions of romantic relationships, unraveling how myths of perfect unions foster unrealistic expectations and emotional turmoil. From romantic comedies that gloss over the complexities of love to the curated images of social media influencers, each element contributes to an idealized vision far removed from reality. This portrayal leaves many dissatisfied when their relationships cannot match these fictional standards. Moreover, consumerism and celebrity culture further entrench these myths by equating material success with relationship fulfillment, blurring the line between genuine connection and superficial displays of affection. Recognizing these influences empowers individuals to challenge societal narratives and embrace the authenticity and imperfection inherent in real-life connections.

Understanding the impact of perfectionism and comparison culture is essential for navigating relationships healthily. The pressure to emulate portrayed ideals fosters dissatisfaction and anxiety, overshadowing the unique dynamics that make each relationship special. By understanding how these expectations shape interpersonal interactions, individuals can appreciate the diversity and complexity of genuine relationships. Cultivating a mindset rooted in self-compassion and authenticity promotes stronger bonds founded on understanding and trust. Encouraging open communication and adaptability allows partners to grow together, moving beyond rigid stereotypes. In doing so, couples can create resilient partnerships capable of weathering life's challenges and being grounded in mutual respect and genuineness—intimacy.

Chapter 2
The Rules Are Rigged

FORCES BEYOND OUR IMMEDIATE awareness often shape perceptions of relationships. Cultural narratives, historical shifts, and economic pressures converge to craft the ideals we accept as the norm in romantic relationships. These influences seep into our consciousness through stories told in fairy tales or seen on screens, frequently portraying love as a flawless and magical journey. However, these perfect depictions can lead to misunderstandings about genuine relationships, overshadowing the effort and dedication required to sustain intimacy. As society continues to indulge in these idealized portrayals, the gap between expectation and reality widens, leaving many feeling unfulfilled and pressured.

This chapter unveils the underlying elements that distort our views of intimacy by delving into how societal standards create unrealistic expectations. This exploration seeks clarity and understanding by examining the role of cultural narratives, economic circumstances' impact, and historical norms' lingering influence. It allows readers to reflect on their perceptions and consider how external factors may shape their experiences and emotions. Ultimately, the chapter aims to encourage a reevaluation of relationship dynamics, fostering authentic connections grounded in empathy, collaboration, and realistic expectations. Through this exploration, readers can arm themselves with insights that allow for healthier, more fulfilling partnerships, guided not by fantasy but by genuine interpersonal growth and understanding.

Cultural Narratives and Economic Influences on Romantic Ideas

In today's world, our perceptions of romance and relationships are sculpted by the compelling narratives we consume daily. These stories, often extensions of cultural and economic forces, mold our ideals and influence how we interact with partners. One predominant narrative is the fairytale trope, which sets unattainable standards, thrusting upon us fantasies that misrepresent genuine relationships. These tales depict a perfect love story, usually culminating in happily-ever-afters while glossing over the inevitable complexities of human relationships.

The notion of an all-encompassing romantic love often takes center stage in these stories, overshadowing the arduous journey couples must undertake. Fairytales glorify idealized versions where conflicts resolve magically, leaving no room for the actual work involved in sustaining a meaningful partnership. This can lead individuals to expect their relationships to mirror these perfectionist ideals, setting them up for disappointment when reality inevitably diverges from fantasy.

Furthermore, these narratives often paint sacrifice as the ultimate expression of true love, equating selflessness with devotion. While compromise is essential, romanticized views of sacrifice can warp this concept into unhealthy dynamics. Many people might feel compelled to disregard their own needs and desires, mistakenly believing that in doing so, they serve a higher purpose in their relationship. Over time, such self-neglect can breed resentment dissatisfaction, and erode the intimacy nurtured within a healthy partnership.

Economically, the pressures faced by couples compound these challenges. Economic strain remains a significant stressor, casting shadows over relationship satisfaction and stability. Financial insecurity can lead to constant tension, making it difficult to focus on nurturing emotional connections. Job instability, the burden of debt, or housing expenses can chip away at the foundation of a partnership, creating an environment where arguments and frustration supersede affection and understanding.

Additionally, wealth disparities introduce complex layers to relationship dynamics. They influence not just individual expectations but also broader societal choices surrounding partnerships. In many societies, there's an expectation that financial stability should precede commitment, leading individuals to delay significant milestones like marriage or starting a family. This becomes particularly pronounced when partners come from different economic backgrounds, potentially fostering unrealistic expectations and societal divides.

Such disparities can perpetuate stereotypes about what constitutes a "suitable" partner based on economic standing. The media's portrayal of affluent lifestyles often reinforces the idea that material wealth is synonymous with happiness and relationship success. This may lead individuals to prioritize financial status over emotional compatibility, inadvertently ignoring the many other factors crucial for long-lasting bonds.

While these cultural narratives and economic factors craft an alluring image of romance, it's critical to step back and question their validity and impact. Individuals can forge more realistic expectations regarding intimate relationships by recognizing the skewed perspectives promoted by fairytales and the distortions introduced by economic pressures. Acknowledging that every couple faces hardships and that genuine love requires continuous effort—beyond grand gestures and idealized sacrifices—is critical to cultivating enduring relationships.

Ultimately, awareness of these influences allows couples to approach their relationships with greater empathy and understanding. It encourages open dialogue, helping partners articulate their needs and navigate challenges collaboratively. As society increasingly emphasizes emotional intelligence and personal growth, this insight becomes invaluable, empowering individuals to redefine their narratives and foster fulfilling, authentic connections grounded in reality.

Historical Context and Media as Perpetuators of Relationship Norms

Throughout history, the institution of marriage has undergone significant transformations. Initially rooted in social and economic contracts, marriage was often a partnership to consolidate wealth, power, or familial alliances. In many societies, love was not the primary factor in these arrangements. However, as cultural and societal norms evolved, so did the concept of marriage. By the 18th century, romantic love began to gain prominence as a legitimate basis for marriage, particularly in Western cultures. This shift from obligation to affection introduced new complexities and pressures. While marrying for love promised personal fulfillment, it also set the stage for ideals that were sometimes difficult to achieve. The notion that one should find everything—love, companionship, support—in a single partner created heightened expectations.

These changes in the foundation of marriage also influenced communication styles and conflict resolution within relationships. Traditional gender roles had long dictated specific expectations for men and women. Men were perceived as the breadwinners tasked with providing for their families, while women were expected to maintain the home and nurture familial bonds. Such roles shaped how couples interacted with one another. Communication was often one-sided, with men making decisions and women following suit. Conflict resolution favored maintaining the status quo, frequently sidelining women's perspectives or concerns. Despite progress towards gender equality in recent decades, the remnants of these historical roles continue to influence how couples communicate today, sometimes hindering open dialogue and equitable partnership.

Moreover, the portrayal of relationships in media has played a pivotal role in shaping contemporary relationship norms. Romantic films, for example, often present idealized narratives that can distort viewers' perceptions of real-life experiences. These films frequently depict grand gestures, unwavering passion, and flawless resolutions to conflicts, perpetuating an unrealistic relationship standard. They tend to gloss over the mundane aspects of a partnership, such as compromise, shared responsibilities, and everyday disagreements, thus fostering false expectations about what a loving relationship should entail. As a result, individuals may find themselves disappointed when their relationships fail to match these cinematic ideals.

In the modern era, social media has further complicated the landscape of intimate relationships. Platforms like Instagram and Facebook allow users to curate their lives meticulously, showcasing only the most attractive, exciting, or romantic aspects. This selective presentation creates a distorted reality where others' relationships appear perpetually perfect, leading to unhealthy comparisons among couples. Partners may feel inadequate or unsatisfied when measuring their lives against these polished portrayals without considering the unseen struggles and imperfections behind the scenes. This constant comparison can generate pressure to conform to perceived norms, straining relationships rather than enhancing them.

Acknowledging these influences is crucial for those seeking genuine connections free from external pressures or misaligned expectations. Understanding marriage's evolution and accompanying challenges allows individuals to define success on their terms rather than subscribing to outdated ideals. Similarly, recognizing the lingering effects of traditional gender roles on communication enables partners

THE GAME YOU CAN NEVER WIN   17

to work towards more equitable interactions, fostering understanding and cooperation. It's essential to view media critically, recognizing romantic films as entertainment rather than accurate representations of relationships. Being mindful of social media's curated nature can help prevent unnecessary comparisons that may detract from personal happiness.

Developing healthier relationship dynamics involves proactive efforts to unlearn these ingrained narratives. Couples might benefit from openly discussing their values and expectations, allowing room for authenticity and growth. Encouraging mutual respect and active listening can bridge gaps left by historical gender roles, creating a space where both partners feel heard and valued. Limiting exposure to idealized portrayals in media, whether through movies or social networks, can reduce undue stress and enable couples to appreciate their unique journey without feeling overshadowed by fiction.

Understanding these broader contexts can also be valuable for mental health professionals and educators working with clients navigating relational complexities. By examining the historical and media-driven factors influencing behavior, they can offer informed guidance, helping individuals break free from societal constraints that hinder self-awareness and emotional intelligence. Professionals can empower clients to establish their definitions of intimacy and fulfillment grounded in reality and mutual understanding.

For those on personal development journeys, this insight provides a foundation for enhancing communication skills and emotional intelligence across various relationships. By questioning mainstream narratives and redefining standards of success, individuals can cultivate meaningful connections based on authenticity, empathy, and collaboration. This process also encourages a broader reflection on how societal structures influence personal beliefs, facilitating growth in romantic relationships and all facets of life.

Final Thoughts

This chapter has delved into the various forces that shape our perceptions of relationships, exploring how cultural narratives and economic realities contribute to unrealistic romantic ideals. By dissecting the impact of fairytales and media portrayals, we see how they paint an overly perfect image of love, ignoring real couples' everyday challenges. Additionally, historical perspectives on marriage reveal layers of expectations that have evolved but continue to influence modern partnerships. Recognizing these influences allows individuals to approach their relationships with healthier expectations, focusing on authenticity rather than fantasy.

Understanding the economic pressures and historical legacies that affect relationship dynamics is crucial for fostering genuine connections. This awareness helps partners engage more openly, addressing individual needs and building a foundation rooted in empathy and collaboration. For those seeking personal growth or assisting others in navigating relational challenges, acknowledging these skewed perceptions can provide more precise insight into achieving emotional intelligence and satisfying partnerships. Individuals can cultivate meaningful, fulfilling relationships grounded in reality by moving beyond societal constraints and redefining success on personal terms.

Chapter 3
Unpacking Myths of Success

MYTHS ABOUT WHAT MAKES a relationship successful can profoundly shape our perceptions and expectations. They often simplify complex dynamics into easy-to-follow, appealing, yet potentially misleading narratives. These myths promise a straightforward path to love and happiness but frequently lead people astray, setting impossible standards that real-life relationships struggle to meet. By confusing duration with success or mistaking initial chemistry for lasting love, these misconceptions create a gap between expectation and reality. This chapter seeks to bridge that gap by unraveling the myths surrounding relationships and helping readers distinguish between superficial measures of success and more profound, meaningful connections.

In this chapter, we will explore various misconceptions that cloud people's understanding of what it truly means to succeed in a relationship. The focus will be on deconstructing the idea that longevity equates to happiness, uncovering how quality over quantity plays a pivotal role in sustaining emotional closeness. By examining societal pressures and traditional success metrics, we'll reveal how they sometimes prioritize appearances over genuine fulfillment. The myth of love at first sight will be scrutinized, showcasing how true compatibility is often mistaken for fleeting passion. Readers will also gain insight into the critical role of emotional labor in maintaining relational balance, providing a comprehensive guide to nurturing authentic connections rather than adhering to romanticized ideals.

Misconceptions of Longevity and Success Metrics in Relationships

In today's society, there is a prevalent belief that the longer a relationship lasts, the more successful it is. This notion equates longevity with happiness, suggesting that couples who stay together have achieved success. However, this association often overlooks the core aspect of fulfillment. Longevity can sometimes mask more profound dissatisfaction within relationships. It's common for couples to remain together out of routine or societal pressure rather than genuine contentment. While these relationships may endure on the surface, they might lack the deep emotional satisfaction that defines genuine connection.

Understanding emotional presence versus mere time spent together is essential in nurturing a lasting bond. Quality time is a concept many are familiar with, yet more superficial metrics like hours clocked often overshadow it. Emotional presence—being genuinely attentive and engaged—nurtures growth within a relationship. Conversely, spending time without real engagement can lead to emotional neglect. Partners may find themselves coexisting rather than truly living together, fostering resentment over time. The duration becomes irrelevant when emotional needs aren't met, showing that it's not about how much time you spend but how you spend it that matters.

Another pitfall of associating longevity with success is the complacency it breeds. When couples rely solely on the length of their relationship as a testament to their success, it stifles motivation for positive change. Without the impetus to strive for improvement, apathy can set in. Effort becomes underestimated, leading to a stagnant partnership where growth is halted. This mindset undercuts the dynamic nature of relationships, which require continuous nurturing and adjustment as both partners evolve.

Societal success metrics further entrench misleading beliefs about relationships. We tend to prioritize external markers such as marriage as indicators of success. While marriage can be a meaningful commitment, elevating it above emotional fulfillment creates disconnects. True success in relationships isn't defined by achieving traditional milestones but by the quality of the emotional bonds shared. When societal metrics overshadow personal fulfillment, individuals might feel pressured into maintaining appearances rather than pursuing genuine happiness.

Refocusing on fulfillment demands a significant shift in perspective. Instead of measuring success by duration, individuals should prioritize understanding what brings true joy and satisfaction within their relationships. This involves setting aside societal expectations and engaging in open and honest dialogues with partners about mutual needs and desires. Couples must embrace the idea that effort and active participation are cornerstones of a thriving relationship, regardless of length. By doing so, partners can forge deeper connections rooted in authenticity rather than fulfilling predetermined societal roles.

Debunking Love-at-First-Sight and Emotional Labor in Relationships

The myth of instant love is persistent in our culture. It is often portrayed in movies and songs as a moment where two individuals lock eyes across a crowded room and immediately know they are meant to be together forever. This notion glosses over the reality of infatuation versus genuine commitment. When people idealize initial attraction, they frequently confuse infatuation with deep love, misinterpreting the spark of excitement as genuine compatibility. Infatuation may feel all-consuming, leading one to believe in an idealized version of the other person without recognizing their full complexity. The idea that love can be instantaneously fulfilling often leads to premature judgments about compatibility, sometimes culminating in unsuccessful long-term commitments.

True love doesn't sprout fully formed; it grows and strengthens through shared experiences. It's within the journey of moving past the first impression that real depth is realized. Whether sharing mundane routines or facing challenges together, these experiences build a foundation that anchors a relationship. Such a foundation emphasizes shifting from craving instant gratification to valuing long-term growth and development. Genuine love appreciates the process, not just the outcome, understanding that lasting connections are crafted patiently through enduring respect and collaboration.

Many are led astray by the illusions of chemistry and its role in relationships. While chemistry, or that initial intense attraction, can be exhilarating, it is crucial to recognize that forming a solid, lasting bond requires more than a rush of emotions or adrenaline. Chemistry often inspires commitments based on the excitement of newness, overshadowing other essential aspects, such as communication and trust, which are fundamental to sustaining any relationship successfully. Genuine relationships require trust built over time, clear and understanding communication, and mutual respect.

A common mistake is assuming that something must be missing if there isn't an immediate sense of fireworks. However, fireworks fade while steady warmth endures. The misconception that passion is synonymous with love can lead individuals to prioritize superficial attributes over substantive qualities, like shared values and future aspirations. Instead, emotional intelligence should guide decisions, enabling partners to see beyond temporary sparks toward more meaningful interactions and intentions.

An overlooked aspect of successful relationships is the concept of emotional labor. Emotional labor includes individuals' unseen efforts to maintain relational harmony and balance. Understanding emotional labor involves recognizing these invisible contributions—such as managing household responsibilities, supporting each other's ambitions, and nurturing an emotionally safe environment—as critical elements for maintaining relational balance. This acknowledgment underscores the appreciation for the tireless work often performed behind the scenes.

In traditional narratives, these efforts go unappreciated because they aren't sensational or easily measurable. Yet, emotional labor is integral to the persistence and intimacy of a partnership. Relational dynamics thrive when both individuals appreciate the unspoken attempts by their partners to enhance their mutual well-being. It requires patience, empathy, and ongoing negotiation to ensure that each person's contributions are visible and valued.

Another facet of emotional labor is the ability to empathize and support a partner during trials. This includes being emotionally available, listening actively, and providing encouragement or comfort when needed. These actions may not be grand gestures but are powerful in reinforcing the connection and cultivating a more profound understanding between partners. Over time, the accumulation of such acts fortifies the relationship's resilience.

Partners need to navigate moments of disagreement with care and understanding. Conflict resolution isn't solely about determining who's right or wrong but rather prioritizing the relationship's well-being. During such conflicts, the strength and quality of communication become profoundly significant. Open dialogue, devoid of judgment or accusation, enables couples to address issues constructively, preserving the affection that brought them together.

Emotional intelligence also plays a vital role in recognizing and addressing one's needs and those of the partner. Often, these needs are subtle and require attentive observation to identify and fulfill them appropriately. By honing the skills to discern and respond to these cues, partners can ensure that their relationship remains attuned to the evolving personal landscapes within their partnership.

The myths surrounding instant love and its misconceptions about romance dictate unrealistic standards that impede authentic connection. Individuals can cultivate more satisfying and enduring relationships by understanding that love is patient, grounded in reality rather than fantasy, and shaped by consistent, invisible efforts. Acknowledging that lasting love requires time, effort, and mutual dedication paves the way for a relationship dynamic where both parties feel seen, understood, and cherished.

Bringing It All Together

In this chapter, we explored the misconceptions shaping our understanding of what makes relationships successful. By dissecting the belief that longevity equates to happiness, we have seen how it can mask deeper issues and lead to complacency. Emotional presence has been emphasized over time, highlighting how genuine engagement fosters authentic connections. We have also examined how societal success metrics, like marriage, can overshadow personal fulfillment, urging couples to redefine success based on mutual satisfaction and open communication.

Moving beyond the myths of instant love and emotional labor, this chapter calls for reevaluating romantic ideals by recognizing the distinction between infatuation and lasting commitment. While chemistry and passion are exciting, we discussed that lasting relationships are built on trust, empathy, and shared values. Understanding and appreciating the role of emotional labor is crucial for maintaining relational harmony. Ultimately, this chapter encourages individuals to invest in their relationships through patience, ongoing effort, and open dialogue, laying the foundation for meaningful and enduring connections.

Chapter 4
Shadows of Superficiality

IN OUR RAPIDLY EVOLVING digital age, the quality of connections between people is shifting significantly. Superficiality seems to be casting its shadow over how we communicate and relate to one another. As technology advances, the way we form bonds changes, often leading to relationships lacking depth and emotional richness. This transformation is especially noticeable in digital interactions, where quick exchanges overshadow meaningful conversations. The allure of staying connected at all times might give an illusion of close relationships, yet it also risks reducing complex human interactions to mere surface-level engagements. This interplay between technology and relationships invites us to reflect on the quality of our connections and consider their impact on our emotional well-being.

This chapter delves into the dynamics of superficial connections in our contemporary society and how they contrast with the deeper bonds essential for enriched relationships. It explores how digital communication shapes our interactions, highlighting the absence of non-verbal cues crucial for understanding emotions and intentions. Furthermore, the chapter examines how social media maintains a curated image that can distort self-perception and affect genuine relationship-building. Readers will be encouraged to reassess their approach to communication by considering more deliberate and patient engagement methods. In doing so, individuals can explore ways to combat the rapid pace of modern life and resist the temptation of instant gratification. The discussion will offer insights into nurturing authentic connections that transcend the shadows of superficiality, promoting emotional fulfillment and relational depth. The chapter aims to guide readers toward cultivating more meaningful relationships in an increasingly interconnected world by addressing these themes.

Digital Communication and Social Media Dynamics

In today's digital age, online communication has fundamentally altered how we interact. While it offers unparalleled convenience and connectivity, it also fosters superficial bonds that can hinder genuine human connections. This shift is primarily driven by the impact of media and how digital communication lacks essential non-verbal cues.

One of the critical elements absent in digital exchanges is non-verbal communication, such as facial expressions, gestures, and body language. These cues are vital for conveying emotions and intentions, allowing us to understand each other deeply. Without these signals, digital conversations often lead to misunderstandings and shallow interactions. For instance, a simple text message lacking tone can be interpreted in various ways, sometimes resulting in unnecessary conflict or confusion.

The mere absence of these cues can foster misunderstandings and shallow exchanges. Recognizing this gap can encourage readers to seek deeper forms of interaction. For those seeking more meaningful connections, it is crucial to complement digital conversations with face-to-face interactions whenever possible, or at least incorporate video calls where visual cues can be better interpreted. Trying to read between the lines and engage in empathetic listening can also bridge the gap left by the lack of non-verbal signals.

Moreover, online communication tends to promote shortened attention spans. The rapid-fire nature of texting and instant messaging rewards speed over substance, often discouraging thoughtful dialogue.

This pattern limits our ability to have profound discussions and fosters a culture of impatience, where individuals become less willing to invest time and energy into nurturing relationships. Engaging in rapid exchanges decreases the likelihood of deeper conversations. Readers will gain insight into the importance of investing time in relational discussions. It encourages readers to embrace patience and dedication by recognizing the value of engaging in more extended, uninterrupted conversations. By setting aside dedicated time for meaningful discourse, individuals can counteract the tendency toward surface-level engagement, leading to more prosperous, more fulfilling connections.

Social media platforms, while connecting people globally, also contribute to the phenomenon of echo chambers. These digital spaces often group individuals with similar beliefs and interests, limiting exposure to diverse perspectives. This restriction can stifle personal growth as users are less likely to encounter differing viewpoints that challenge their ideas. In relationships, this dynamic can inhibit authentic communication and self-reflection, making it difficult for individuals to expand their horizons and deepen their understanding of others. Readers may identify how this limits their relational expansion and authenticity. Challenging one's own beliefs through diverse interactions fosters more profound experiences. Engaging in diverse conversations, seeking out differing opinions, and embracing diverse communities can help break free from echo chambers and enrich one's perspective.

Furthermore, the pressure to manage one's image on social media significantly impacts how individuals perceive connections and view themselves. The constant need to curate an idealized version of oneself online can create unrealistic expectations and distort self-worth. People often compare their real lives to the polished images others present, leading to feelings of inadequacy and dissatisfaction. This inflated perception of connection can make it challenging to form genuine relationships, as individuals may prioritize maintaining a perfect digital image over authentic self-expression.

When perceived connections differ from real-life interactions, readers benefit from remembering the disparity. Exploring offline activities and fostering self-esteem independent of digital validation can lessen the psychological strain tied to online personas. Adopting digital detoxes or periodically stepping back from social media can also aid in reassessing priorities, leading to more authentic online and in-person relationships.

Impact of Instant Gratification and Fast-Paced Lifestyles

In today's fast-paced world, the culture of instant gratification permeates nearly every aspect of our lives, significantly impacting how we form and maintain relationships. This pervasive need for immediate satisfaction often undermines the patience and commitment essential for building solid and meaningful connections. In many ways, society's shift towards wanting everything now is eroding our capacity to engage deeply with one another, overshadowing genuine emotional needs that take time and effort to fulfill.

The quest for instant gratification can be compared to a quick fix—it provides temporary pleasure but lacks the sustaining qualities necessary for long-term fulfillment in relationships. For example, dating apps allow us to connect with potential partners within seconds based solely on first impressions without taking time to know someone honestly. This approach encourages surface-level interactions, where individuals focus on short-term enjoyment rather than laying the groundwork for a lasting connection. The rush to achieve romantic milestones can overlook the gradual process of relationship building, which is fundamental to fully understanding and appreciating each other.

Furthermore, modern lifestyles characterized by constant busyness further compromise the depth of our connections. People today often juggle multiple responsibilities simultaneously, leaving little time or energy to devote to nurturing relationships. This hurried pace leads to mindless interactions, where engagements are more transactional than meaningful. Conversations become mere exchanges of information rather than opportunities to explore thoughts and emotions. The velocity at which life moves prevents us from being present in our interactions, thereby diminishing the quality of our connections.

The pressure to maintain busy schedules reduces interaction quality and results in neglecting significant relational moments. Important events like anniversaries, family gatherings, or simple daily rituals like shared meals become lost in ceaseless activities. These moments cultivate a sense of belonging and intimacy; their absence can create feelings of isolation or dissatisfaction. When we prioritize tasks over people, relationships suffer, depriving them of the attention and acknowledgment required to thrive.

We might consider taking inspiration from nature to counteract this trend. Unlike the rapid pace of modern living, nature unfolds gradually in cycles that teach us the value of patience and endurance. Just as most natural phenomena progress slowly, healthy relationships require time to flourish. By allowing space for growth and development, we can appreciate the nuances of our partnerships rather than rushing through them in search of immediate rewards.

Setting realistic expectations around communication can also help manage the impact of instant gratification on relationships. In an age where replies are expected instantaneously, it may be beneficial to establish boundaries regarding response times. Communicating openly with partners about these boundaries can reduce misunderstandings and help prevent the anxiety of waiting for a reply. Slowing down and engaging more intentionally promotes a more profound understanding, fostering stronger connections.

Moreover, acknowledging the detrimental effects of a fast-paced lifestyle and the allure of instant gratification creates opportunities to make conscious changes. Introducing technology-free zones or times within our daily routines can provide the mental space to focus on interpersonal relationships. Engaging in activities that require presence, such as outdoor walks or shared hobbies, can reinforce relational bonds by offering shared experiences and memories.

Concluding Thoughts

In today's rapidly evolving digital landscape, this chapter explored the impact of superficial connections on meaningful interactions. It highlighted how the absence of non-verbal cues in digital communication often leads to misunderstandings, suggesting that incorporating face-to-face interactions or video calls can bridge this gap. Additionally, it addressed how the pace and brevity of online exchanges discourage profound dialogue, urging readers to invest time in nurturing deeper conversations. By emphasizing patience and commitment, individuals can foster more fulfilling relationships despite the challenges posed by technology.

The chapter also delved into the societal pressures of instant gratification and fast-paced lifestyles, revealing how these factors undermine genuine connections. Recognizing the tendency towards surface-level interactions prompted by quick fixes like dating apps and social media, the text encouraged a shift toward embracing slow, intentional relationship-building. It urged readers to create space for meaningful engagements, set realistic communication expectations, and establish technology-free zones to enhance relational depth.

Through these efforts, individuals can cultivate enduring connections free from the constraints of modern digital habits.

Chapter 5
Breaking Free from Expectations

BREAKING FREE FROM expectations is an endeavor that taps into our deepest desires for authenticity and fulfillment. It challenges us to confront the invisible strings that societal norms often use to map out the pathways of our relationships. How do we distinguish between what enriches our lives and merely complies with external ideals? This exploration invites readers to pause and evaluate the motivations behind their relational choices, encouraging them to listen more intently to the whispers of their values. Here lies an opportunity for introspection and courage—embracing personal truth as a foundation for relationships rather than following well-trodden but perhaps unsatisfying paths laid out by tradition or peer pressure.

This chapter opens up a discussion about recognizing and resisting social expectations' subtle yet pervasive influence on our connections with others. Readers will delve into practical strategies for asserting their unique values while navigating societal pressures. There will be an emphasis on identifying core values as a compass for decision-making, maintaining personal boundaries, and fostering environments where authentic self-expression is supported and celebrated. It offers insights into building supportive networks that champion individuality over conformity. From the power of reflective practices to seeking like-minded communities, each segment addresses crucial tools for cultivating genuine, value-based relationships. Together, these elements form a compelling narrative that helps individuals strengthen their self-awareness and ties with others, leading to more prosperous, more satisfying relational experiences grounded in genuine understanding and respect.

Resisting Peer Pressure and Defining Personal Values

To break free from societal expectations, it's crucial first to recognize the power of peer influence on our relationship choices. Social pressure can subtly dictate how we believe relationships should look and function, often leading us away from our authentic desires. Many conform to norms without consciously realizing it, hindering genuine self-expression and personal satisfaction in relationships. Understanding this influence involves examining how perceptions shape peers, media, and cultural narratives. By acknowledging these forces, individuals can start setting boundaries that protect their core values.

Setting boundaries is an essential strategy for upholding personal values amidst social pressures. It requires courage to assert one's beliefs, especially when they clash with societal or peer expectations. For example, a couple might face pressure to marry or have children based on age-old societal norms, even if it goes against their current life goals. Setting boundaries enables them to navigate such pressures by reaffirming their commitment to what truly matters to them. This protects the integrity of their relationship and fosters deeper personal fulfillment.

Developing strategies for asserting individual beliefs involves focusing on authenticity and self-preservation. Authenticity means staying true to oneself, even when external opinions suggest otherwise. Self-preservation in social settings includes cultivating the ability to say "no" respectfully but firmly when situations arise that conflict with personal values. For instance, if an individual feels pressured to compromise their relationship standards because "everyone else is doing it," this approach allows them to maintain integrity. Assertiveness training can be beneficial here, offering tools and techniques to express needs and boundaries confidently.

Reflective practices are powerful tools for uncovering and defining core relationship values independently from societal trends. These practices can include journaling, meditation, or regular self-assessment activities designed to explore what genuinely brings happiness and peace in relationships. Through reflection, individuals identify what values and qualities they seek in relationships beyond superficial measures dictated by society. This introspection helps distinguish between what one truly desires and what is expected, fostering deeper connections grounded in mutual respect and understanding.

Building connections with individuals who support authenticity rather than impose societal norms is vital for sustainable personal growth. True friends uplift and encourage individuality, understanding that each person's path is unique. These supportive networks provide safe spaces where expressing one's authentic self is encouraged and celebrated. People find strength and reassurance by surrounding themselves with like-minded individuals through friendships, communities, or supportive groups. There is less fear of judgment in these environments, allowing for more honest communication and connection.

Identifying personal values is another critical guideline for prioritizing values over societal norms. Personal values act as a compass, guiding decisions and fostering resilience against external pressures. To identify these values, individuals might ask fundamental questions about what makes them feel fulfilled and purposeful in relationships. Reflecting on past experiences where they felt most aligned with their true selves can provide insightful cues. Additionally, considering role models or influential figures who embody qualities they admire can further clarify these values. Once identified, these values can consistently guide actions and decisions, helping maintain alignment with one's true self even when faced with opposing societal expectations.

Building a supportive network is equally important and is a practical tool for resisting negative peer influence. This involves actively seeking out friendships and communities that celebrate diversity and authenticity. Engaging in environments that embrace varied perspectives enriches one's understanding of relationships and affirms that there is no singular way to experience them. Joining clubs, groups, or online communities focused on shared interests or values can offer this support. These connections reinforce the notion that prioritizing personal values over societal pressures leads to more authentic and satisfying relational experiences.

Building Self-Esteem and Cultivating Resilience Against Judgment

Cultivating intrinsic self-esteem becomes essential in an era where societal pressures often define our sense of self-worth. Understanding the distinction between internal and external validation is a critical first step in this journey. External validation comes from others' recognition, approval, or acknowledgment of our actions or attributes—often acting as a fragile, unstable foundation for self-esteem. Conversely, intrinsic self-esteem, grounded in personal values and beliefs, provides a more resilient and enduring sense of self-worth.

Intrinsic self-esteem is about valuing oneself irrespective of external accolades or criticisms. It requires shifting focus from how others perceive us to how we see ourselves. For instance, instead of seeking praise for professional accomplishments from colleagues, a person with intrinsic self-esteem might find satisfaction in knowing they have done their best work, aligned with personal goals and values. This form of self-esteem not only fosters confidence but also helps individuals remain anchored amidst the fluctuating opinions of others.

To foster intrinsic self-esteem, practicing self-compassion is vital. Self-compassion involves treating ourselves with the same kindness, empathy, and understanding that we would offer a dear friend. A practical way to begin this practice is through self-affirmations and optimistic internal dialogue. Affirmations such as "I am worthy" or "I am enough" can be powerful tools in reshaping one's self-narrative and counteracting self-critical thoughts. Positive internal dialogue encourages us to replace negative self-talk with constructive and supportive conversations with ourselves.

Another aspect of self-compassion is recognizing our shared humanity and acknowledging that imperfection is part of being human. By accepting our flaws without harsh judgment, we open the door to embracing ourselves fully, imperfections and all. Visualize extending compassion towards oneself during a challenging moment, asking, "How would I support a friend experiencing this?" Such practices nurture a compassionate inner voice, reinforcing our sense of worth independent of external circumstances.

Overcoming dependence on external validation involves celebrating personal milestones and growth. Often, individuals measure success by comparing themselves to others, leading to feelings of inadequacy. Instead, focusing on personal achievements—even small victories—can significantly enhance self-esteem. For example, finishing a challenging project or learning a new skill should be celebrated without comparing it to others' accomplishments. This shift in perspective allows individuals to appreciate their unique journeys and progress.

Celebrating personal milestones helps build an internal metric of success based on individual growth rather than societal standards. One forms an airtight narrative around internal motivations and goals by acknowledging personal efforts, like maintaining a fitness routine or successfully managing a work-life balance. Over time, these celebrations reinforce an individual sense of value and accomplishment independent of outside validation.

Analyzing the origins of judgments that impact our self-esteem is equally essential. The quest for external approval is often rooted in past experiences or deeply ingrained beliefs about oneself. Mindfulness practices play a crucial role here, enhancing awareness of our thoughts and emotions without becoming overidentified. Observing these mental patterns allows individuals to identify when they seek external validation and explore underlying reasons.

Cognitive restructuring is another powerful tool for developing emotional resilience. It involves challenging negative thought patterns and replacing them with more balanced views. For instance, if someone feels inadequate after social media comparisons, cognitive restructuring would encourage them to reframe their perspective, focusing on their strengths and potential instead. This process of reframing narratives is transformative, promoting a healthier self-image.

They are creating supportive environments that further aid in building emotional resilience. Surrounding oneself with individuals who uplift and encourage genuine self-expression can diminish the reliance on external validation. These relationships provide a safe space to explore vulnerabilities without fear of judgment. They foster a sense of belonging, essential for nurturing intrinsic self-esteem.

While breaking free from societal expectations is no small feat, the transformative power lies in developing a deep, unwavering belief in one's worth. Individuals cultivate this belief and experience profound personal growth and greater relationship fulfillment. Ultimately, the journey toward intrinsic self-esteem is a dynamic and continuous process. It requires patience and persistence but promises a life enriched with authenticity and self-acceptance.

Bringing It All Together

This chapter sheds light on resisting societal pressures to create authentic relationships aligned with personal values and self-acceptance. By examining how peer influence shapes our perceptions, we've explored strategies for setting boundaries and asserting beliefs. Reflective practices help identify core relationship values, allowing individuals to differentiate between their desires and societal expectations. The idea is to cultivate connections where authenticity thrives, surrounding oneself with supportive networks that embrace individuality.

As we conclude, the emphasis is on nurturing a deep connection with one's inherent worth. This involves redefining success and fulfillment based on internal metrics rather than societal standards. Celebrating personal achievements builds a robust self-esteem rooted in resilience against external judgment. Such approaches pave the way for more meaningful and satisfying relationships. Ultimately, breaking free from limiting norms leads to a fulfilling life characterized by genuine connections and self-discovery.

Chapter 6
Navigating Emotional Costs

NAVIGATING THE EMOTIONAL costs of relationships involves recognizing the hidden toll that unrealistic expectations can exert on personal well-being and relational health. In modern society, countless individuals are trapped in cycles driven by comparison and fear of judgment. Such patterns are subtle yet pervasive, often going unnoticed until they manifest as emotional exhaustion or anxiety. The quest for perfection manifests as self-imposed demands and societal pressures that dictate how one should conduct romantic affiliations. These pressures silently shape interactions, leading individuals to prioritize external validation over authentic connections. From social media influences to cultural norms, the craving for acceptance becomes a driving force that propels people into an endless pursuit of approval.

Within this chapter, readers will explore the profound impact of constant comparisons on their lives, especially in social interactions and digital engagement. It delves into the ways these comparisons foster anxiety and alter behaviors, highlighting how the desire to avoid judgment often leads to performative actions rather than genuine exchanges. Moreover, the discussion extends to neglecting personal needs and identity in pursuing approval, illuminating the emotional drain and disconnection from prioritizing others' expectations. Through exploring these dynamics, the chapter sheds light on invisible sacrifices made behind public facades and how striving to meet perceived standards can skew authenticity. Practical insights guide breaking free from these patterns, emphasizing the importance of self-reflection, direct communication, and gratitude practices. Ultimately, this chapter aims to equip readers with tools to recognize and address the emotional costs, fostering healthier, more fulfilling relationships.

Burnout from Constant Comparison and Anxiety from Fearing Judgment

In the realm of modern relationships, emotional fatigue and anxiety often stem from constant comparisons and fear of judgment. Many individuals are caught in an exhausting cycle, perpetually measuring their relationships against others'. This relentless comparison can result in a profound sense of unfulfillment, leaving individuals and couples less satisfied with their connections.

Social media plays a pivotal role in amplifying these feelings of inadequacy. Platforms like Instagram and Facebook present a curated reality—highlight reels that often distort genuine experiences. People portray idealized versions of their lives, showcasing moments of happiness and success while concealing struggles and imperfections. As a result, observers may feel isolated and inadequate, and their relationships may appear lackluster by comparison. This skewed perception can lead to increased isolation as individuals withdraw from real-life interactions, feeling their authentic selves are insufficient.

Moreover, the fear of judgment can lead people to alter their behavior, creating a facade to protect themselves from criticism. Relationships become performative rather than authentic as partners strive to present an image that aligns with perceived social standards. These modifications can erode trust and intimacy, essential to any healthy relationship. When interactions are driven by the desire to be perceived positively by others, the genuine connection between partners suffers. Authenticity gives way to a game of appearances, draining emotional resources and diminishing satisfaction.

Anxiety further compounds these issues when individuals become overly attuned to external feedback. Every comment, like, or reaction on social media can trigger stress, keeping individuals on edge about how they are perceived. This constant need for validation imposes significant pressure, diverting attention from meaningful communication within the relationship. Partners begin to focus more on managing perceptions than fostering honest dialogue. Over time, this creates a barrier to genuine connection, weakening relational bonds.

Neglect of Self in Pursuit of Approval and Invisible Sacrifices Behind Public Facades

Navigating the emotional landscape of relationships, especially when self-neglect is involved, can be complex and draining. Individuals often find themselves prioritizing their partners' needs over their own, damaging their emotional well-being and identity. This dynamic creates a fertile ground for resentment. When someone consistently puts another's desires ahead of their own, they may feel undervalued or invisible, eroding self-worth. This imbalance, often stemming from an earnest desire to maintain peace or gain approval, ultimately leads to dissatisfaction and frustration (Short, 2024).

Such behavior sets off a cyclical pattern where seeking approval becomes an endless loop. Initially, this might manifest as small sacrifices or compromises, but gradually, it consumes more emotional resources. The constant need for validation saps one's energy, rendering them emotionally exhausted and detached. This disconnection not only affects the individual's mental health but also disrupts the harmony in relationships, making genuine connections challenging (Rose, 2023).

Facades present another layer of complexity. To meet what they perceive as expected standards, individuals may hide their true selves, masking insecurities and vulnerabilities. This effort to present an idealized version of themselves is exhausting and unsustainable. Over time, maintaining such facades results in burnout, impacting relational dynamics by skewing authenticity and openness. Partners are left interacting with a constructed persona rather than the individual behind it, leading to misunderstandings and unmet needs.

Societal pressures heavily influence these behaviors, reinforcing that vulnerability equates to weakness. In many cultures, there's an unspoken expectation to uphold certain appearances in personal relationships. These pressures discourage honest discussions, prompting individuals to maintain facades even when it's detrimental. As a result, meaningful dialogue about struggles and challenges becomes rare, further entrenching the cycle of disconnection. The lack of vulnerability not only stifles emotional growth but also hampers the establishment of healthy boundaries. The absence of openness fosters an environment where misunderstandings flourish, and trust diminishes.

Guidelines to counteract these patterns involve conscious self-reflection and mindful engagement in relationships. Encouraging individuals to reflect on their values and what brings them joy can foster a sense of fulfillment. Understanding one's intrinsic worth, independent of others' opinions, establishes a strong foundation for healthy interactions.

Promoting gratitude practices can cultivate an appreciation for unique relational experiences. Acknowledging and celebrating distinct moments shared with loved ones helps shift focus from external validation to internal satisfaction. This practice diminishes the power of societal expectations and enhances one's ability to appreciate authentic connections.

Suggesting regular digital detoxes offers a practical way to mitigate exposure to comparative stimuli. Individuals can focus on developing genuine interactions free from unrealistic benchmarks by stepping away from social media and other comparison-driven platforms.

Moreover, establishing clear communication channels allows for the sharing thoughts and feelings without fear of judgment. This involves listening actively and expressing concerns honestly, paving the way for deeper understanding and empathy. Such dialogue is crucial in creating balanced partnerships where both parties feel valued and heard.

Mental health professionals and educators are vital in supporting individuals in navigating these challenges. Providing resources and guidance can help clients recognize unhealthy patterns and develop strategies to foster healthier relational dynamics. Encouraging open discussions about societal pressures and the impact of maintaining facades can empower individuals to make informed choices about their behaviors and interactions.

Final Insights

In this chapter, we've delved into the emotional expenses tied to pursuing perfection in relationships, examining how unrealistic expectations can quietly burden individuals and partnerships. The exploration highlighted the roles that comparison, fear of judgment, and facade maintenance play in eroding genuine connection and satisfaction. These factors contribute to a cycle of self-neglect and perceived inadequacy, often amplified by social media and societal pressures. It's evident that these patterns not only strain personal well-being but also compromise relational health. Acknowledging these dynamics is crucial for fostering relationships rooted in authenticity and mutual understanding.

The narrative encourages us to reflect on our values and what truly brings joy, emphasizing the importance of internal fulfillment over external validation. Suggestions like practicing gratitude, engaging in digital detoxes, and establishing open communication channels offer practical ways to nurture healthier relational dynamics. Mental health professionals and educators are essential in guiding individuals through these challenges, offering resources to build resilient connections. By breaking down facades and embracing vulnerability, we can cultivate relationships where partners feel valued, heard, and genuinely connected.

Chapter 7
Redefining Success

REDEFINING SUCCESS within relationships requires a shift in focus, challenging the prevailing societal norms that often equate achievement with perfection. This transformation invites individuals and couples to explore a more nuanced understanding of success that prioritizes growth, mutual fulfillment, and adaptability over rigid benchmarks. By recognizing that imperfections are a natural part of human bonds, this approach encourages a more profound connection where authenticity is valued above all. Instead of chasing an imaginary ideal, partners can engage in meaningful experiences emphasizing personal growth, nurturing vulnerability, and celebrating small victories. This perspective reshapes how we perceive and measure achievements within our intimate partnerships, ensuring they align with individual values rather than external pressures.

In this chapter, readers will delve into how embracing imperfections sets the stage for more prosperous, rewarding relationships. The narrative explores the pivotal role of vulnerability as a foundation for trust and empathy, demonstrating its strength in fostering genuine intimacy. Alongside this, the text examines growth dynamics, illustrating how personal and relational development go hand-in-hand, reinforcing each other at every step. The chapter guides readers on navigating life's changes together through practical insights, showcasing adaptability as a critical factor in sustaining partnership resilience. It also sheds light on redefining success through personalized metrics, urging couples to create milestones that resonate with their unique journey. Moving away from conventional success indicators, the chapter invites couples to forge their path, highlighting the importance of shared goals and flexible definitions of accomplishment. Ultimately, this exploration offers valuable tools for cultivating a fulfilling relationship that thrives on understanding, shared growth, and mutual satisfaction.

Embracing Imperfections and Valuing Growth

One profound shift in redefining success within relationships lies in accepting imperfections and moving the spotlight from tangible achievements to valuing growth. This transformation begins with the understanding that the notion of a "perfect" relationship is an unrealistic construct. Society often portrays perfection in relationships through various media, painting images of romantic partnerships devoid of flaws. However, this pursuit of flawlessness can prevent genuine intimacy from flourishing, as it places unnecessary pressure on partners to meet unattainable standards.

Recognizing imperfections as inherent to the human experience allows partners to breathe more easily within their relationships. Instead of striving for an impossible ideal, couples can focus on authentic connections and shared journeys. Through these perceived flaws, individuals find opportunities to connect at a deeper level, fostering intimacy and understanding. Accepting imperfections dismantles the facade of perfectionism, making room for something far more valuable: vulnerability.

Vulnerability, often misunderstood as a weakness, is a cornerstone of solid relationships. Embracing one's flaws and those of a partner invites vulnerability into the relationship space, which is essential for trust to flourish. When partners are vulnerable, they open the door to empathy and compassion. Sharing fears, insecurities, and unpolished truths paves the way for mutual support. In doing so, relationships gain resilience, allowing partners to navigate challenges together rather than standing apart in times of stress or crisis.

Moreover, seeing growth as an asset rather than a point of contention is pivotal in reshaping relationship dynamics. Relationships are not static entities; they evolve as individuals grow and change over time. Acknowledging that personal development and relational growth occur concurrently encourages partners to view each other as ever-evolving beings. This perspective fosters continual discovery, transforming potentially stressful transitions into opportunities for strengthened bonds.

For example, navigating a career change can pose significant stress, yet when both partners commit to seeing growth as a shared journey, they create an environment where resilience thrives. This adaptability ensures that partners support each other's aspirations while nurturing the relationship's broader horizon. Recognizing growth as a positive force aligns with the understanding that relationships must accommodate personal transformations, creating a foundation of ongoing mutual appreciation.

Further contributing to this redefined vision of success in relationships is flexibility in defining accomplishments and milestones. Traditional metrics of relationship success, such as financial stability or social status, often rely heavily on external validations. Moving beyond these conventional measures towards personal achievements and shared goals encourages a more fulfilling relationship experience.

In practice, this might mean celebrating small victories that align with personal values, like developing better communication habits or working through a challenging disagreement constructively. These moments foster a sense of accomplishment without succumbing to societal pressures. They underscore the importance of recognizing individual and collective achievements, illustrating that success in a relationship does not have to mirror societal expectations but should resonate personally with both partners.

Adopting this flexible approach helps partners to establish criteria that honor their unique bond, setting realistic and meaningful milestones. It also creates a framework where both partners feel validated in their individual pursuits and collective endeavors, reinforcing the relationship as a supportive alliance rather than a competitive dynamic.

Fostering Mutual Satisfaction and Adaptability

Relationships are dynamic and multifaceted, requiring a delicate balance between personal fulfillment and mutual growth. Achieving this harmony is integral to maintaining a healthy partnership. At the core of these relationships lies the ability to communicate openly. Open dialogue ensures both partners can express their needs and sustain satisfaction over time. When couples engage in healthy conversations about what they require from each other, it minimizes misunderstandings and fosters a more profound connection. These discussions should not be seen as periodic check-ins but rather as ongoing dialogues that evolve with the relationship.

A frequent obstacle in relationships is the confusion between needs and wants. Understanding this distinction is crucial for any successful partnership. Needs are essential elements such as emotional support, respect, and love that form the foundation of the relationship. On the other hand, desires are more flexible and may change over time. These could range from aspirations like career advancement to hobbies and lifestyle changes. Recognizing that desires can evolve allows partners to effectively support each other's transitions and changing interests. This mutual understanding helps prevent conflicts when one partner feels their needs are not being met due to conflicting desires.

As life progresses, change is inevitable, and embracing these changes together can significantly strengthen a relationship. Whether it's adapting to new jobs, moving to a new city, or navigating parenthood, learning to negotiate these changes collaboratively reinforces the concept of teamwork. It reduces anxiety as partners know they have each other's backs, thus reaffirming the importance of addressing both parties' needs. This adaptability acts as a buffer against the fear of change, transforming potential stressors into opportunities for partnership strengthening.

Moreover, building collaborative problem-solving skills is critical to sustaining long-term relationships. Allocating dedicated time to address potential hurdles allows couples to work through obstacles as a team. This act of problem-solving highlights a shared commitment to the relationship's success, fostering trust and highlighting each partner's investment. For example, setting aside a regular meeting to discuss financial planning or future goals shows an active effort to tackle issues head-on rather than letting them fester. This proactive approach resolves current problems and equips the couple with skills to handle future challenges, making the relationship resilient over time.

Cultivating a growth mindset within relationships is vital for nurturing a thriving partnership. Encouraging each other's personal development and celebrating achievements, no matter how small creates a culture where growth is valued over static accomplishments. It shifts the focus from merely existing within the framework of a relationship to thriving together, continuously evolving as individuals and partners. This mindset aligns with adaptability, reinforcing that change isn't just accepted but welcomed as a means of mutual enrichment.

Adaptation in relationships isn't merely a survival tool but a strength that underpins resilience. In practice, this means viewing changes not as disruptions but as chances to grow closer. By adopting an adaptable attitude, couples can use challenges as stepping stones, inevitably increasing the robustness of their connection. For instance, adjusting expectations during stressful life phases, such as a career change or family illness, turns a potentially divisive issue into a unifying experience. In this way, adaptability becomes a testament to the relationship's health and resilience.

Concluding Thoughts

Throughout this chapter, we've delved into redefining relationship success by embracing imperfections and valuing growth. This shift from traditional ideals of perfection allows partners to focus on authentic connections and mutual journeys. Acknowledging that imperfections are a natural part of the human experience enables relationships to thrive with genuine intimacy and understanding. By welcoming vulnerability, couples create an environment for trust and empathy, strengthening their bonds to navigate life's challenges together. Furthermore, growth is recognized as an asset, encouraging partners to see each other as evolving individuals and transforming change into opportunities for a deeper connection. As they adapt to life's transitions, couples can support each other's aspirations while nurturing their shared relationship goals.

We also explored the significance of mutual satisfaction and adaptability in fostering relationships. Communication is pivotal here, fostering open dialogues that address needs and desires without confusion. Recognizing which aspects of our partnerships are essential and which are malleable helps minimize misunderstandings and encourages mutual growth. Embracing changes together, whether related to career moves or life events, strengthen partnership resilience and teamwork. Collaborative problem-solving further underscores a shared commitment to a thriving relationship, fostering trust and equipping couples with skills to handle future challenges. This chapter highlights that adaptability isn't just about survival but is a testament to a healthy, resilient, and fulfilling relationship.

Chapter 8
Authenticity Over Perfection

STRIVING FOR AUTHENTICITY in relationships can often feel like navigating a complex maze, yet it holds the key to forming deep and meaningful connections. In a world where perfection is frequently idolized, embracing genuine expression may seem counterintuitive. Nonetheless, authenticity fosters an environment rich with trust and understanding by encouraging individuals to share their true selves and create bonds based on sincerity. This chapter unpacks how prioritizing authenticity over faultlessness can transform interactions from superficial exchanges into profound experiences, ultimately leading to more satisfying relationships.

Throughout the chapter, readers will explore the importance of cultivating honesty as the foundation of any genuine relationship. It delves into the dynamics between partners when truth-telling becomes a shared value, discussing how vulnerability serves as a bridge to empathy and connection. Insightful examples illustrate the ripple effects of honesty, highlighting the destruction that deception and pretense can inflict upon a bond. Furthermore, the text investigates the challenges one may encounter while practicing authenticity, offering strategies to navigate these hurdles effectively. By examining real-life scenarios, the chapter underscores the growth opportunities presented by embracing vulnerability and hints at the rewards of deeper intimacy and unwavering trust. As you continue this journey, you'll discern actionable insights on how candid communication leads to stronger romantic relationships and enriches interactions across various spheres of life.

Honesty as Foundation

Honesty is the cornerstone of authentic relationships. By embracing truth-telling, individuals can create a haven for intimacy and meaningful connections. When we share our true selves—personal stories, vulnerabilities, and emotions—with others, we lay the foundation for trust and understanding. This act of openness strengthens existing bonds and invites others to be equally honest, fostering a reciprocal environment of sincerity.

In intimate relationships, truth-telling allows partners to feel safe and secure. It's an invitation to be vulnerable, acknowledging strengths and weaknesses without fear of judgment or rejection. For instance, when one partner opens up about past experiences, they demonstrate trust in their significant other, encouraging similar openness in return. This mutual exchange of truths cultivates a more profound connection rooted in authenticity rather than perfection.

Trust, born from honesty, is essential for building robust relationships. Once trust is established, it becomes easier for people to understand each other's needs and desires. This transparency promotes empathy and compassion when partners communicate openly about their feelings, aspirations, and fears. An example might involve one partner expressing anxiety about a career change; by sharing this concern honestly, they invite support and reassurance from their partner, deepening their bond through shared understanding.

The absence of honesty, however, can have detrimental effects on relationships. Even minor fabrications or omissions can erode trust over time. These seemingly insignificant lies can lead to misunderstandings and emotional distance. For example, if someone consistently downplays their frustrations to avoid conflict, these hidden feelings can fester, undermining the relationship's integrity.

Dishonesty disrupts the harmony necessary for genuine connection, as it hides one's true self behind a facade of deceit.

Building a culture of honesty within relationships is crucial to prevent such adverse outcomes. Establishing ground rules for open communication is a vital step in this process. Partners should agree to be transparent with one another, addressing any issues or concerns promptly rather than allowing them to escalate. This can be achieved by setting aside regular times to talk openly about the relationship and its dynamics, allowing each person to voice their thoughts and feelings in a supportive setting.

Celebrating candid sharing is another way to reinforce openness and honesty. When individuals acknowledge and appreciate each other's truthfulness, it encourages further sincere exchanges. Simple acts, such as offering gratitude when a partner shares their emotions or supporting them after they've shown vulnerability, can go a long way in reinforcing this culture of honesty. By valuing truth-telling, couples prioritize authenticity over perfection in their relationships.

Building such a culture doesn't happen overnight—it requires ongoing effort and commitment from both parties. However, the benefits are profound. As individuals become more comfortable being truthful, they help dismantle the barriers of deception and fear, creating a space where love and intimacy can flourish. This fosters a sense of belonging and acceptance, where partners feel seen, heard, and valued for who they are.

Building Trust through Vulnerability

In today's fast-paced world, pursuing perfection often overshadows the deeper connections we crave in relationships. However, vulnerability, not perfection, becomes the secret ingredient to fostering meaningful bonds. Embracing one's vulnerabilities can lead to a more profound sense of trust and intimacy between individuals, fundamentally altering the dynamics of any relationship. By understanding and practicing vulnerability effectively, we create an environment where empathy thrives, and authentic connection is possible.

Vulnerability is an invitation for empathy. When one opens up about their true feelings, challenges, and insecurities, they allow others to see them as they are. This sharing creates deep empathy and understanding opportunities, making both parties feel seen and heard. For instance, consider how much of communication is non-verbal; acknowledging that over 55% of communication relies on body language underscores the importance of genuine engagement with another's emotional state ("Intimacy and Safety – Your Life. Your Story. Your Journey.", 2018). When someone feels safe to express themselves without fear of judgment, a strong foundation of emotional safety ensues, setting the stage for trust and closer intimacy.

Effective vulnerability practices become essential to promote authentic exchanges. These include expressing emotions openly, actively listening, and sharing personal stories. Expressing emotions doesn't mean airing every grievance or complaint but being honest about how specific actions or words impact you. Active listening, on the other hand, involves giving your full attention, avoiding judgment, and validating the emotions shared by your partner. Simple actions like maintaining eye contact and offering supportive body language indicate that you care about what is being communicated ("Intimacy and Safety – Your Life. Your Story. Your Journey.", 2018). Sharing stories, whether about past experiences or current challenges, also helps humanize us in the eyes of others, breaking down perceived barriers and encouraging reciprocal vulnerability.

However, facing the challenges that come with vulnerability is inevitable. The fear of rejection or misunderstanding often discourages people from revealing their true selves. But these very challenges provide fertile ground for growth and evolution within relationships. Acknowledging these fears openly allows partners to address and overcome them collectively, transforming such experiences into stepping stones toward deeper intimacy. It's important to remember that being vulnerable isn't about exposing weaknesses; it's about showing strength in transparency. The courage to share our inner lives is what fosters resilience against life's adversities (*How Vulnerability Helps Build Trust and Intimacy in a Relationship*, n.d.).

Guidelines for facing these challenges can be simple yet powerful. First, recognize that vulnerability is a shared journey, not a solo quest. Both partners should commit to supporting each other through this process. Equally crucial is the nurturing of an empathetic space where judgments are suspended. Whenever difficult emotions arise, both should practice patience and understanding, discussing fears openly instead of retreating behind walls. Reinforcing your commitment to work through challenges together, rather than using exit language, ensures a safe atmosphere ("Intimacy and Safety – Your Life. Your Story. Your Journey.", 2018).

Real-life stories show that those willing to embrace vulnerability often transition from superficial relationships to ones rich with depth and connection. Consider the story of a couple who, after years of avoiding sensitive topics, incorporated regular "check-in" times into their routine. During these sessions, they would take turns expressing gratitude for each other's efforts, acknowledge struggles throughout the week, and reassure each other of their commitment to growing together. Over time, this practice led to them not only feeling more supported but also more deeply connected. Their willingness to engage in vulnerable conversations became a catalyst for transforming their relationship from one of routine interactions to one characterized by a profound emotional bond.

This narrative demonstrates that vulnerability does not guarantee immediate transformation but requires persistence and mutual dedication. Success stories emerge when couples or individuals in any relationship dynamic leave their comfort zones and face the discomfort of sincerity. In doing so, they redefine their bonds, shifting from surface-level interactions to more meaningful engagements built upon honesty and acceptance.

Ultimately, inviting vulnerability into relationships is akin to embarking on a journey of rediscovery. It requires patience and a willingness to confront uncomfortable truths. The rewards, however, are invaluable—deeper trust, greater intimacy, and a stronger connection with those around us. By transforming the fear of vulnerability into an opportunity for growth, individuals are better equipped to forge lasting, impactful relationships that transcend societal pressures of perfection.

Final Insights

As we've explored, authenticity is the linchpin for nurturing meaningful relationships transcending the need for perfection. Embracing truth and vulnerability builds trust and intimacy, highlighted by genuine communication and understanding. In romantic connections and beyond, sharing our true selves facilitates empathy and compassion, creating an environment where deeper emotional bonds can flourish. Mutual openness encourages partners to support each other's journeys, reinforcing that authenticity is more valuable than any facade of flawlessness.

This chapter underscores the transformative power of honesty within human interactions, inspiring individuals to prioritize sincerity over pretense. Authentic exchanges invite a sense of belonging, ensuring everyone feels valued for who they indeed are. By embracing the courage of vulnerability, relationships evolve into profound experiences filled with appreciation and acceptance. The journey toward authenticity might be ongoing, but its rewards—trust, connection, and lasting emotional resonance—make it undeniably worthwhile for those seeking more profound, more fulfilling relational dynamics.

Chapter 9
Developing Emotional Intelligence

DEVELOPING EMOTIONAL intelligence is vital to forming more profound and more meaningful connections with others. While many recognize its importance, understanding how to cultivate this skill can be challenging and requires intentional effort. With the right approach, anyone can enhance their emotional intelligence by focusing on essential areas that facilitate better personal and professional relationships.

This chapter explores several crucial aspects of emotional intelligence, beginning with understanding personal emotions and practicing empathetic listening. We delve into identifying emotional triggers and how to manage them effectively. The significance of using an extensive emotional vocabulary is also highlighted, as it allows for more transparent communication and helps prevent misunderstandings. By validating emotions, we create a supportive environment that encourages open dialogue and strengthens interpersonal bonds. Additionally, the chapter examines how mindfulness, interpreting non-verbal cues, and developing response plans contribute to effective emotional management. Through practical methods such as journaling, reflecting on past experiences, and observing contextual clues, readers will gain insights into refining their emotional intelligence skills for improved interactions in various settings.

Understanding Personal Emotions and Practicing Empathetic Listening

Emotional intelligence (EI) is essential for developing self-awareness and building strong emotional connections with others. It begins with recognizing emotional triggers, which can dramatically impact our emotional responses. Understanding these triggers allows us to create a buffer between stimulus and response, effectively preventing knee-jerk reactions that might lead to conflict or misunderstandings. For example, consider how a heated discussion at work might trigger feelings of inadequacy due to past experiences. Recognizing this trigger lets you consciously choose a more measured response rather than reacting impulsively, thus fostering healthier interactions.

To further deepen emotional bonds, active listening plays a pivotal role. When we listen actively, we fully understand not just the words but also the emotions behind them. This practice builds trust and signals to the speaker that their feelings and thoughts are valued. Active listening involves maintaining eye contact, nodding in agreement, and asking clarifying questions. Doing so makes the speaker feel respected and understood, paving the way for meaningful discussions. Imagine confiding in a friend who attentively listens to your worries without interrupting or judging; such exchanges strengthen emotional ties and create space for vulnerability and authenticity in relationships.

A critical component of communicating effectively within emotional intelligence is employing a diverse emotional vocabulary. Being able to name and articulate emotions precisely reduces the potential for misunderstandings. Many people are familiar with basic emotions like happiness, sadness, or anger, but delving into nuanced descriptions such as 'anxious anticipation' or 'frustrated resignation' can significantly enhance mutual understanding. Accurate articulation allows individuals to express their feelings clearly, leading to better support from others and more effective problem-solving within personal and professional settings. For instance, telling a colleague you feel 'overwhelmed by pressure' rather than just 'stressed' provides context about your situation, enabling them to offer targeted assistance.

In conjunction with accurate expression, validating emotions is paramount for cultivating an atmosphere of emotional safety and open communication. Validation does not mean agreeing with another's feelings but acknowledging their right to those feelings. A simple statement like "I can see why you'd feel that way" can have a profound effect, allowing people to feel heard and understood. This acknowledgment encourages openness, as individuals become more willing to share their fears, anxieties, or joy without fear of judgment or dismissal. In family dynamics, when parents validate their children's emotions, they empower them to communicate more openly and honestly, thereby nurturing emotionally intelligent future adults.

Identifying emotional triggers, journaling emotions, and reflecting on past experiences are practical methods to bolster self-awareness and master personal emotional landscapes. These practices serve as guidelines for individuals seeking to refine their EI skills. Identifying emotional triggers requires introspection—consider moments of intense emotional reactions and dissect what stimuli caused them. Journaling emotions offers a safe space to explore these feelings, providing insights into repeated patterns or unexpected emotional responses. Reflecting on past experiences helps individuals understand how historical events influence current emotional states. This reflection also facilitates personal growth and empathy towards others' emotional struggles.

Distinguishing Between Feelings and Reactions and Interpreting Non-Verbal Cues Effectively

In developing emotional intelligence, one critical aspect is crafting thoughtful, emotional responses and honing non-verbal communication skills. These elements enhance our ability to connect with others on a deep level, creating a pathway to more meaningful relationships. To embark on this path, mindfulness, understanding body language, creating a response plan, and observing contextual clues play vital roles.

Mindfulness is a foundational practice that allows individuals to become keenly aware of their emotions before these feelings translate into reactions. We cultivate a heightened sense of emotional clarity by engaging in mindfulness techniques, such as meditation or simply taking a moment to breathe deeply. This practice helps identify emotions early, preventing them from escalating into reactive behaviors. For example, pausing during a heated conversation to acknowledge one's frustration can diffuse tension and lead to a calmer interaction. Mindfulness empowers individuals to approach situations with balance, ultimately enhancing their emotional intelligence.

Understanding body language is another essential component, offering insights into unspoken feelings and emotions. Often, words can be deceptive or limited in expressing true sentiments. Individuals can decode underlying emotions that might remain hidden by paying attention to gestures, facial expressions, posture, and eye contact. Recognizing when someone avoids eye contact or crosses their arms can signal discomfort or insecurity. Interpreting these signals fosters deeper connections by allowing us to respond appropriately. Such awareness can prevent misunderstandings and facilitate more empathetic interactions with others.

Creating a response plan represents a proactive strategy for managing difficult emotional situations. By envisioning various scenarios and preparing potential responses, individuals can navigate challenging interactions with greater ease and accountability. A response plan might include simple steps like taking a few deep breaths before responding or rehearsing key phrases to communicate clearly under pressure. This preparation supports emotional regulation and instills confidence in handling future situations. It converts impulsive reactions into deliberate responses, thereby fostering more constructive communication.

Observing contextual clues is crucial for understanding emotions and facilitating thoughtful communication. Contextual clues encompass the environment, social dynamics, and previous interactions that shape the current scenario. In any situation, these clues provide valuable information about what might influence someone's behavior or emotions. For instance, in a work meeting, understanding the context of an individual's recent workload could explain a terse response. They are being attuned to such nuances, formulating considerate replies, and adjusting one's communicative approach. This depth of perception enhances emotional intelligence by promoting compassionate and effective dialogue.

Integrating these aspects into daily life requires conscious effort and practice. To develop thoughtful emotional responses, it's essential to routinely reflect on personal emotional patterns and triggers. Journaling experiences and associated emotions can offer insights into recurring themes or areas needing improvement. Additionally, seeking feedback from trusted friends or mentors can help identify blind spots and refine emotional responses.

Incorporating regular mindfulness practices into one's routine further strengthens emotional awareness. Allocating time each day for activities like meditation, yoga, or mindful walking encourages ongoing reflection and self-discovery. Over time, these practices increase one's capacity to pause, assess, and choose optimal responses to emotional stimuli.

Mastering the art of interpreting body language demands consistent observation and study. Engaging in role-play scenarios, attending workshops on non-verbal communication, or watching videos on body language can enhance one's ability to pick up on subtle cues. Practicing these skills in various settings solidifies understanding and boosts confidence in applying this knowledge in real-life situations.

Developing a reliable response plan involves envisioning common emotional challenges and brainstorming solutions. This dynamic planning process should allow adjustments based on new experiences or changing circumstances. Periodic review and refinement ensure the plan remains relevant and practical.

Finally, cultivating the habit of observing contextual clues enriches emotional comprehension and communication. Make a habit of scanning environments, acknowledging social cues, and appreciating past experiences that might influence the present. This broader perspective facilitates nuanced understanding and more thoughtful relational exchanges.

Insights and Implications

As we bring this chapter to a close, let's reflect on how enhancing our emotional intelligence can transform how we connect with others. By gaining insight into our emotions and recognizing what triggers them, we learn to manage our reactions more thoughtfully. This understanding not only helps us maintain calm and avoid misunderstandings but also allows us to form deeper connections. Active listening and validating emotions reinforce these bonds by promoting trust and openness in communication. These skills are essential as they enable us to express ourselves clearly and understand others better, fostering an environment where authentic relationships thrive.

Developing emotional intelligence goes beyond managing personal feelings; it involves interpreting non-verbal cues and contextual clues that enrich our interactions. Being mindful of our surroundings, understanding body language, and planning our responses empower us to handle complex emotional situations gracefully and empathetically. Regular practice, such as journaling or engaging in mindfulness activities, enhances our ability to respond thoughtfully rather than impulsively. By integrating these practices into daily life, we embrace a path toward more meaningful and fulfilling relationships, challenging superficial connections to deepen our mutual expectations and more genuine bonds with those around us.

Chapter 10
Communication: Beyond Words

COMMUNICATING EFFECTIVELY requires more than just exchanging words; it encompasses understanding and interpreting the messages conveyed beyond verbal expressions. In our everyday interactions, we often focus on what is being said rather than how it is said, missing out on underlying non-verbal cues and emotional undertones that significantly influence relational dynamics. Mastering communication involves diving deeper into these intricacies, allowing for a richer exchange of thoughts and emotions that fosters profound connections. As individuals, recognizing and valuing the importance of these unseen elements can transform our relationships, making them more meaningful and satisfying.

This chapter explores various methods that enhance communication beyond spoken language. It starts with understanding active listening and its role in reducing misunderstandings by fully engaging with the speaker's words and emotions. We delve into conflict resolution strategies, emphasizing the importance of expressing personal feelings using 'I' statements to avoid defensiveness and blame in disagreements. Reflective listening is discussed as a crucial component in showing empathy and connecting through shared understanding. Additionally, the chapter examines non-verbal communication, highlighting how body language, facial expressions, and physical touch convey messages of support or discomfort. The narrative covers how open-ended questions can deepen conversations by inviting comprehensive responses and how structured approaches can help resolve recurring disputes. By the end of this chapter, readers will have a toolkit of skills and insights necessary for nurturing relationships based on genuine understanding and collaboration, steering away from superficial interactions towards enduring bonds built on mutual respect and empathy.

Active Listening and Conflict Resolution

Enhancing relationships requires more than just talking—it demands active and attentive listening and effective conflict-resolution techniques. By honing these skills, individuals can create more robust, more fulfilling connections that are not just based on what is said but on how it is perceived and understood.

Active listening is an essential practice in improving relationship dynamics. This technique involves being fully present and attentive to your partner, allowing them to express themselves without interruption. When we truly listen, we validate the speaker's feelings and experiences, which helps reduce misunderstandings. For example, when a partner discusses a challenging day at work, active listening might involve maintaining eye contact, nodding in understanding, and resisting the urge to offer solutions immediately. This presence allows both partners to explore their emotions profoundly and encourages a more genuine dialogue.

A key component of active listening is reflective listening. This involves summarizing or paraphrasing what the other person has expressed. Doing so demonstrates focus and comprehension, which fosters trust within the relationship. For instance, if one partner articulates feeling overwhelmed by responsibilities, the listener might respond, "So you're feeling stressed because of the many tasks you have to manage?" Such reflections affirm the listener's understanding and encourage the speaker to clarify unspoken emotions or thoughts. Reflective listening acts as a bridge that connects hearts through shared knowledge.

Equally crucial in healthy communication is the use of 'I' statements during conflicts. These statements help create a non-defensive atmosphere by centering discussions around personal feelings rather than accusations. Instead of saying, "You never listen to me," one might phrase it as "I feel unheard when our conversations seem one-sided." This approach promotes mutual understanding and avoids placing blame, making it easier for both parties to discuss their needs openly. 'I' statements shift the conversation from pointing fingers to expressing personal experiences, reducing defensiveness and opening up possibilities for constructive dialogue.

Resolving conflicts also necessitates creating follow-up plans, ensuring that issues are fully addressed and communication remains ongoing. After a disagreement, it's beneficial for partners to agree on a strategy that revisits the problem later, allowing time for reflection and emotional cooling-off. For instance, after concluding a heated discussion, partners might decide to revisit the topic at a specific time, ensuring each has the opportunity to voice lingering thoughts or emotions. This planning is crucial as it affirms the commitment to resolve differences and nurtures a continuing dialogue, anchoring the relationship in collaboration and respect.

Moreover, staying present during conversations enhances understanding and reduces miscommunication. Being mentally and emotionally present means giving undivided attention to the speaker and acknowledging their words intellectually and emotionally. In a fast-paced world of distractions, remaining focused during intimate dialogues conveys value and importance to the partner, fostering a deeper connection. Presence is critical in minimizing interruptions and facilitating a safe space where both partners can freely share.

While implementing these strategies, it is crucial to ask open-ended questions. Such inquiries invite comprehensive responses that promote richer conversations. Questions like "How was your day?" can be expanded into "What was the most challenging part of your day?" This slight modification encourages elaboration and shows genuine interest, strengthening relational bonds. Open-ended questions propel dialogues that reveal insights, perspectives, and feelings that might otherwise remain unspoken.

To practically apply these methods, consider a scenario where partners face recurring disagreements about household responsibilities. Practicing active listening would involve sitting together without distractions and attentively hearing each other's viewpoints. Reflective listening can be used to verify understanding: "It sounds like you feel overburdened by chores—is that correct?" The 'I' statements would be as follows: "I feel stressed when I come home to a messy house." Finally, they could create a follow-up plan, perhaps setting aside time weekly to reassess chores and responsibilities. This structured approach ensures that feelings are acknowledged, problems are discussed respectfully, and solutions are collaboratively sought.

Non-verbal communication and Expressing Needs

In communication, non-verbal cues are vital in conveying messages beyond spoken words. A vast array of unspoken interactions occur within our relationships daily, and these interactions can be as powerful, if not more so, than verbal exchanges. These cues often reveal unspoken intentions and their sincerity, ultimately enhancing openness and receptiveness in relationships.

Understanding body language is crucial for interpreting these unspoken signals. How we move, stand, or even the expression on our faces can communicate volumes about our true feelings and intentions. For instance, maintaining eye contact might suggest attentiveness and interest, while averting one's gaze could imply discomfort or disinterest

(Segal et al., 2018). Becoming more attuned to these subtle signals allows for more genuine interactions, as both parties can better sense sincerity and openness in each other's actions.

Moreover, physical touch and gestures like hugs or holding hands are powerful tools for expressing affection and support. These actions transcend the limitations of verbal communication, offering comfort when words fail. A simple gesture, such as a hand on the shoulder, can convey empathy and understanding without uttering words (Scharlop, 2018). These moments of connection through physical touch reinforce bonds and strengthen emotional ties by providing a sense of reassurance and solidarity.

While understanding non-verbal cues is essential, articulating personal needs effectively is equally important within any relationship. Discussing needs clearly can prevent misunderstandings and foster an environment of open communication. Positive framing plays a key role here; presenting one's needs positively rather than focusing on what's lacking encourages collaboration and understanding rather than defensiveness. Saying, "I feel more at ease when we have our alone time together," instead of "You never spend time with me," puts the focus on a shared desire rather than blame.

Negotiation and compromise are also fundamental to healthy relationships. They demonstrate respect for each individual's values and perspectives. This mutual respect allows both parties to find a middle ground, strengthening partnerships and promoting commitment. For example, choosing a holiday destination together involves weighing each person's preferences and making compromises—perhaps alternating years for selecting the destination ensures fairness and mutual satisfaction. Couples can forge stronger connections that withstand challenges over time by honoring each other's perspectives.

Empathizing with one another enhances these dynamics further. Empathy requires acknowledging the other person's feelings and experiences, creating more profound understanding and compassion. When partners genuinely empathize, their communication becomes more heartfelt and meaningful. They listen actively and respond thoughtfully, fostering an emotional connection that resonates well beyond words. This practice nurtures the relationship, ensuring each partner feels valued and understood.

Assessing situations calmly before addressing conflicts is another critical aspect of effective communication. Taking time to cool down ensures emotions remain controlled, preventing heated arguments that can lead to hurtful exchanges. Calmer assessments allow individuals to approach sensitive topics rationally, paving the way for constructive discussions rather than explosive confrontations. This approach helps maintain harmony, even during disagreements, by prioritizing understanding over winning an argument.

Using "I" statements when discussing issues frames feelings and needs from a personal perspective. This avoids placing blame or making accusations, which can trigger defensiveness. Instead of saying, "You make me upset when you're late," rephrasing to "I feel worried when you're late" focuses on expressing personal emotions while avoiding pointing fingers. Such statements promote honest dialogue, encouraging both parties to express themselves openly without fear of exacerbating tensions.

Finding common ground is another technique that proves invaluable during disagreements. Focusing on shared values and goals enables couples to navigate through differences effectively. Individuals can avoid contentious issues by identifying areas of agreement and instead collaborate towards mutually beneficial solutions. This unity fosters a sense of partnership, allowing for growth and development as a team rather than adversaries.

Lastly, establishing follow-up conversations provides opportunities to revisit complex conflicts after initial discussions. Sometimes, resolving intricate problems may require multiple sessions before reaching conclusions. Designating times to talk again shows a commitment to working things out collaboratively and underscores the importance of continuous communication. Follow-ups encourage ongoing exploration of unresolved matters, reinforcing dedication and care for the relationship's well-being.

Final Insights

The chapter has delved into communication, emphasizing the importance of verbal and non-verbal skills in fostering deeper connections. It highlighted how active listening and conflict resolution can enhance relationship dynamics by encouraging empathy and understanding. Effective active listening involves being present and attentive, using techniques like reflective listening to validate the speaker's feelings. Conflict resolution requires employing 'I' statements to express personal emotions instead of casting blame, promoting healthy dialogue that focuses on mutual understanding and respect. Additionally, follow-up plans ensure ongoing discussions, allowing partners to refine their communication strategies for a harmonious relationship continuously.

Beyond spoken words, non-verbal communication has been explored as a vital aspect of expressing sincerity and emotions. Understanding body language and physical gestures can convey messages that words cannot fully capture. The significance of articulating personal needs clearly without blame was also discussed to prevent misunderstandings and encourage collaboration. Negotiation, compromise, and empathy are essential tools for nurturing lasting partnerships. By framing needs positively and assessing situations calmly before addressing conflicts, individuals can maintain harmony and create a stronger bond. Together, these skills equip us with the means to build more profound, satisfying relationships that transcend societal norms and superficial interactions, aligning with our deepest emotional needs.

Chapter 11
Fostering Mutual Growth

FOSTERING MUTUAL GROWTH in relationships involves nurturing connections that allow both individuals to evolve and thrive. It is about creating a dynamic where both partners support each other's aspirations while embracing their changing identities. This concept of shared development is not just ideological but practical, providing a solid foundation for more robust, resilient partnerships. The essence of such relationships lies in understanding that when two people grow together, they build a bond adaptable to life's various challenges.

This chapter explores how establishing shared goals can significantly enhance relationship dynamics. Readers will learn the importance of setting joint objectives aligning with individual values and future visions. The chapter delves into practical strategies like using the SMART criteria to ensure clear and achievable goals and fostering teamwork and accountability. Regular check-ins and open communication help partners maintain momentum and adaptability, offering opportunities for reassessment and celebration of milestones. Real-life examples illustrate the journey of couples who have successfully integrated these practices into their lives, highlighting the benefits of celebrating achievements and maintaining individuality within a partnership. Through these narratives, the chapter aims to provide readers with actionable insights into building more fulfilling and sustainable relationships.

Establishing Shared Goals

In fostering mutual growth within relationships, setting joint goals is a powerful way to strengthen partnerships and deepen commitment. By developing shared objectives, partners create a framework supporting collective achievement and individual aspirations. This approach fortifies teamwork and enhances accountability, constructing a united effort toward confronting life's challenges. Through clear goal-setting, couples develop a solid foundation for their future.

One effective method for cultivating joint goals is implementing SMART criteria, which stands for specific, measurable, achievable, relevant, and time-bound. This framework provides clarity and structure, minimizing ambiguity in relationship expectations and increasing the likelihood of achieving desired outcomes. When partners agree on specific objectives, they know precisely what they're working towards. Having measurable goals allows them to track progress, evaluate success, and stay motivated. Ensuring achievable goals means considering each partner's abilities and resources so the targets are realistic yet challenging. Relevance ensures that goals align with the couple's values and long-term vision while being time-bound creates a sense of urgency and facilitates timely completion (<i>SMART Goal Examples to Empower Your Team</i>, n.d.).

Regular check-ins maintain momentum and foster commitment to these shared goals. These meetings allow partners to assess their progress, realign their efforts, and make necessary adjustments. During these conversations, partners can openly discuss obstacles, celebrate achievements, and modify plans. Regular communication ensures that both partners remain aligned and engaged, preventing misunderstandings and promoting cooperative problem-solving.

It's essential to provide room for feedback and adaptability during these check-ins. Encouraging open dialogue about what's working and what isn't helps partners feel heard and respected, strengthening their bond. Flexibility in approaching these goals demonstrates a willingness to support one another's unique needs and evolving aspirations over time. This ongoing engagement fosters a dynamic partnership built on trust and understanding.

Reaching milestones together is an exhilarating part of pursuing joint goals, and celebrating these achievements contributes significantly to relational satisfaction. Each milestone represents a victory shared between partners, reinforcing their unity and dedication. Celebrations don't have to be extravagant; they can be simple acts of acknowledgment that appreciate the effort and commitment to reaching a goal. This recognition builds a culture of appreciation within the relationship, encouraging partners to continue investing emotionally and practically in their shared journey.

Celebrating reinforces positive behaviors and highlights the contributions of both partners, making them feel valued and appreciated. Moreover, when individuals feel supported and recognized, they are more likely to remain committed and motivated to work towards future shared objectives. This cycle of achievement and celebration propels the relationship forward, continuously enhancing connection and intimacy.

To illustrate the importance of setting joint goals, consider Amy and Mark, a couple who decided to save money for a dream vacation. Together, they set a SMART goal: save $5,000 in six months by cutting unnecessary expenses and contributing a fixed amount from each paycheck. They established monthly check-ins to review their spending, reassess their budget, and celebrate small savings milestones.

Amy and Mark became more financially disciplined and collaborative as they worked towards their goal. Their regular check-ins provided opportunities to communicate effectively about finances, which had previously been a source of tension. When they finally reached their target and booked the vacation, the sense of accomplishment was amplified by the shared effort it took to get there. The trip became a symbol of their unity and perseverance, deepening their bond.

Couples like Amy and Mark can reinforce their partnership and commitment in meaningful ways by setting joint goals and following the SMART criteria guidelines. The process allows partners to face challenges together, celebrate successes, and build a stronger, more resilient relationship. Such intentional efforts enrich their immediate interactions and lay the groundwork for enduring harmony and growth.

Nurturing Independence and Adaptability

In a world that often glorifies partnership unity, it's crucial to remember the value of maintaining our individuality within relationships. Encouraging personal interests outside the relationship supports self-discovery and enriches the partnership with diverse experiences and insights. Pursuing their passions offers them a sense of purpose and fulfillment independent of their partner. This autonomy prevents dependency and brings new perspectives into the relationship.

Consider, for example, how exploring new activities like joining a book club or taking up solo sports can invigorate personal and shared spaces in a relationship. These activities provide individuals with opportunities for growth and learning, which they can share with their partners, sparking fresh conversations and interactions. By integrating these personal experiences into the partnership, both individuals contribute to a dynamic, evolving connection that thrives on variety and mutual respect.

Achieving a balance between togetherness and autonomy is key to avoiding feelings of suffocation. Relationships are often associated with closeness, yet too much proximity can lead to an overwhelming sense of being stifled. In contrast, allowing room for autonomy fosters individual growth and rejuvenates relational dynamics. This balance ensures that while partners grow as individuals, they continue to grow together. It's a delicate dance that involves understanding when to lean in and when to step back, something best navigated through open communication.

Open communication during life transitions is vital in navigating change collaboratively. Partners who talk openly about their hopes, fears, and expectations during such times create a foundation of resilience. For instance, moving to a new city might bring excitement and stress. Partners can develop strategies that address personal and shared goals by discussing the potential challenges and adjustments required. This form of transparent dialogue minimizes misunderstandings and helps partners align their paths amidst any upheavals.

In Source 1, a couple learned this firsthand when transitioning to living together ('to, 2015'). They highlighted the importance of stepping back and reflecting individually, which allowed them to identify and tackle minor issues that had begun to disrupt their harmony. This example underscores how essential it is to recognize and voice feelings honestly; it ensures no one feels isolated or misunderstood during periods that demand adaptation.

Creating shared rituals during transitions provides continuity and comfort, strengthening the emotional bonds between partners. Shared rituals could be simple acts like weekly dinners or walks or more involved activities like joint projects or travel plans. Having these well-established routines offers an anchor amid life's uncertainties. Such rituals promote bonding, create a comforting sense of predictability, and act as reminders of unity, providing reassurance even as everything changes.

For example, attending a workshop or retreat together can serve as both a break from routine and a shared experience, deepening the connection through learning and discovery(<i>How to Navigate Major Life Transitions as a Couple</i>, n.d.). Embracing these rituals allows the partnership to evolve, accommodating both partners' shifting identities and aspirations.

Navigating this path effectively helps maintain flexibility and adaptability. Life does not always unfold as planned, and transitions can present unpredictable challenges. Being open to revisiting and adjusting established norms allows couples to navigate changes with grace, highlighting the necessity of fluidity in balancing individual pursuits with collective commitments.

As relationships progress, respecting individuality and fostering togetherness shouldn't just be occasional considerations—they should weave through the fabric of the partnership. Balancing these elements helps create a supportive environment where each partner feels valued and understood as a separate entity and an integral part of a couple. The willingness to pursue interests separately translates into more affluent, more fulfilling companionship.

Final Thoughts

This chapter has explored the importance of nurturing relationships that encourage shared growth and evolving identities. Partners can create a supportive framework for their collective achievements and personal aspirations by setting joint goals.

SMART criteria provide a clear structure, helping couples stay focused and motivated while working towards these goals. Regular check-ins strengthen this partnership by offering moments to celebrate progress, realign efforts, and adapt to each other's needs. Such practices ensure that partners remain committed and engaged, reinforcing their unity through shared objectives and mutual appreciation.

Emphasizing individuality alongside a strong partnership leads to a more resilient relationship. Encouraging personal interests outside the relationship fosters self-discovery and brings fresh perspectives into shared experiences. Balancing independence with togetherness allows partners to avoid feelings of suffocation while maintaining closeness. Open communication during transitions helps navigate changes together, creating strategies that honor individual and shared goals. As couples embrace flexibility and adaptability, they build an environment where each partner feels valued as independent and vital to the union. Together, these efforts lay the foundation for deeper, more satisfying connections.

Chapter 12
Defining Boundaries

DEFINING BOUNDARIES is a cornerstone of nurturing healthy and balanced relationships. Establishing clear limits around personal space, emotional needs, and time commitments helps individuals navigate their connections with others. These boundaries are essential frameworks that allow us to protect ourselves while fostering respectful interactions. Without them, people may feel overwhelmed or misunderstood, leading to unnecessary stress or tension within their relationships. Individuals can ensure that their partnerships remain supportive and enriching by understanding and setting appropriate boundaries.

This chapter will explore the significance of boundaries within relationships, focusing on how they contribute to self-care and emotional well-being. Readers will gain insights into different types of boundaries, such as physical, emotional, and time-related, each playing a unique role in personal interactions. Strategies for establishing these limits effectively, including self-reflection and clear communication, will be discussed to enhance relational dynamics. Moreover, guidance on respecting and handling a partner's boundaries will underscore the importance of mutual appreciation and trust. Lastly, the chapter will address boundary violations constructively and the role of forgiveness in rebuilding trust, providing a comprehensive guide to fostering healthier and more fulfilling relationships.

Establishing and Communicating Personal Limits

Establishing and effectively communicating personal boundaries is vital in maintaining healthy relationships. Recognizing the importance of these boundaries is essential for self-care, emotional well-being, and fostering respectful relationship dynamics. Personal boundaries act as protective measures that define acceptable behavior and safeguard our mental and physical health. Setting boundaries helps individuals establish their personal space and assert themselves, ultimately leading to more balanced interactions.

The concept of boundaries can be broadly classified into different types: physical, emotional, and time-related. Physical boundaries involve the tangible aspects of our lives, such as personal space and physical touch. They are crucial in defining how comfortable we are with physical interaction from others, whether it be a handshake, hug, or more intimate contact. Understanding and expressing your physical limits ensures comfort in personal and professional settings.

On the other hand, emotional boundaries involve protecting personal feelings and thoughts. They delineate emotional responsibilities by ensuring that you do not take on the emotional burdens of others unnecessarily. Emotional boundaries empower people to openly communicate what they find acceptable for their emotional health without feeling guilt or obligation. By maintaining these limits, one can prevent undue stress and emotional exhaustion.

Time boundaries focus on allocating personal commitments and priorities. These boundaries help carve out time for work, leisure, family, and self-care, ensuring a balanced lifestyle. Saying no to tasks that interfere with personal time can prevent burnout and overcommitting oneself. Time boundaries enable individuals to manage their schedules effectively and uphold personal commitments, thus protecting their time and energy.

Self-reflection plays a crucial role in establishing these boundaries effectively. Taking the time to evaluate one's needs and preferences aids in identifying personal limits. This process involves introspection and an honest assessment of what triggers discomfort or dissatisfaction. Self-awareness becomes essential in pinpointing areas where boundaries may be required. Through reflective practices, such as journaling or meditation, individuals can gain clarity on their true desires and fears, paving the way for more authentic interactions.

Once personal limits have been identified, the next step is communication. Straightforward and assertive communication is fundamental in conveying boundaries to others. It's crucial to articulate your needs confidently yet empathetically, ensuring that others understand your perspective without feeling attacked or rejected. For instance, when explaining that you need uninterrupted weekends, framing it around personal rejuvenation rather than avoiding social invitations makes it easier for others to comprehend and respect your decision.

Listening actively to others' responses is also vital in this communication process. Active listening allows for a two-way conversation where both parties feel heard and acknowledged. This reciprocal understanding enhances mutual respect and reinforces relational norms. By engaging in open discussions and reiterations, misunderstandings can be prevented, and relationships strengthened through shared expectations and respect.

However, setting and communicating boundaries is not a one-time exercise; it requires ongoing evaluation and adjustment. As relationships evolve, so too might the boundaries that govern them. Regular check-ins with yourself and others ensure that boundaries remain relevant and practical. If a particular boundary is repeatedly challenged, revisiting the initial reasons for establishing it can offer insights into necessary changes or reaffirmations.

In situations where boundaries are crossed, addressing the issue promptly helps maintain integrity and trust within the relationship. Initiating calm and thoughtful conversations can clarify misunderstandings and reset boundaries. It's essential to approach such dialogues with empathy and a willingness to listen, fostering an environment where both parties feel supported in their journey towards healthier interactions.

Finally, navigating the complex dynamics of power in relationships is another facet where boundaries are significant. Whether dealing with authority figures at work, partners, or family members, understanding the influence of power can guide the appropriate assertion of boundaries. In situations where power imbalances exist, seeking external support, such as counseling, may be beneficial to navigate and communicate boundaries more effectively.

Respecting and Handling Partner's Boundaries

In establishing healthy relationships, recognizing and respecting boundaries is essential for building trust and fostering mutual appreciation. Boundaries serve as the invisible lines that define limits in interactions, safeguarding individuality while promoting a secure and supportive environment. By honoring a partner's boundaries, we affirm their autonomy and create a safe space where both individuals can thrive.

A fundamental aspect of boundary maintenance is differentiating between needs and demands. Needs refer to essential elements required for emotional well-being, such as respect and understanding, whereas demands often arise from expectations or pressures that might lead to obligations or resentment. Individuals can foster compassionate interactions that prioritize emotional health over fulfilling burdensome requirements by focusing on needs rather than demands. For instance, if a partner expresses the need for personal time when feeling overwhelmed, acknowledging this need without perceiving it as a demand prevents miscommunication and nurtures empathy within the relationship.

Handling boundary violations gracefully requires thoughtful strategies that emphasize open communication and commitment to solutions. When a boundary is crossed, responding with clarity and composure is crucial. Utilizing "I statements" can aid in this process by framing feelings and reactions in a non-confrontational manner. For example, saying, "I feel hurt when my personal space isn't respected," enables constructive dialogue without placing blame directly on the other person. This approach paves the way for honest discussions about why a violation occurred and how it impacted both parties involved.

Equally important is the commitment to actionable change following these discussions. Addressing boundary breaches must go beyond mere apologies; it involves genuinely understanding the underlying issues and implementing changes to prevent recurrence. Partners can work together to establish guidelines for future interactions, ensuring that both individuals feel heard and valued. This collaborative approach resolves immediate conflicts and strengthens relational bonds by demonstrating a shared commitment to growth and mutual respect.

Forgiveness plays a vital role in rebuilding trust after boundaries have been violated. Recognizing that everyone has flaws and mistakes allows room for understanding and reconciliation. Offering forgiveness does not imply condoning harmful behavior but signifies a willingness to move forward with renewed trust and openness. It acknowledges the potential for positive change and is a step toward healing relational wounds.

Moreover, cultivating an environment that encourages regular reflection on personal boundaries is crucial for preventing future violations. Individuals should practice self-awareness, regularly evaluating their boundaries and communicating any necessary adjustments to their partners. This proactive approach ensures that boundaries remain relevant and respected as circumstances evolve.

In scenarios where boundary violations occur frequently, despite efforts to address them, seeking external support from a counselor or therapist may be beneficial. Professional guidance can provide neutral insights and facilitate productive conversations between partners, aiding them in understanding one another's perspectives more deeply and exploring viable solutions collaboratively.

To sustain healthy boundaries, both partners must also respect their own limits. Self-respect is foundational to upholding boundaries, preventing individuals from compromising their well-being to avoid conflict or pleasing others. By asserting personal limits respectfully and consistently, individuals can model boundary-setting behaviors for their partners, promoting a culture of mutual respect within the relationship.

Ultimately, maintaining boundaries involves ongoing effort and intentional practice. As relationships grow and change, so must the boundaries that protect their integrity. By embracing open communication, empathy, forgiveness, and adaptability, individuals can create lasting partnerships grounded in trust and mutual appreciation. Relationships strengthened by these principles will endure challenges and flourish in an atmosphere of respect and unwavering support.

Constructively recognizing and addressing boundary violations is vital for nurturing healthy relationships characterized by trust and mutual appreciation. Honoring a partner's boundaries affirms individuality and creates a secure, supportive environment. Differentiating between needs and demands fosters compassion by prioritizing emotional well-being over obligations or resentment. Effective strategies for handling boundary violations, like the clear articulation of feelings through "I statements," promote understanding and collaboration in finding solutions. Forgiveness and actionable change are crucial for restoring trust after boundary breaches and facilitating relational resilience through comprehension and growth.

Guidelines for clear communication are integral to this process. Individuals should strive for calmness and clarity when discussing boundary violations selecting an appropriate time to communicate feelings and concerns. Using "I statements" simplifies expression while avoiding accusations, allowing for a constructive exchange of emotions and intentions. By engaging in open dialogue and emphasizing respect, partners can work together to prevent future infractions, thereby enhancing relational trust.

Final Thoughts

This chapter delved into the vital role boundaries play in cultivating healthy relationships, emphasizing the importance of recognizing and respecting individual limits. By establishing boundaries, individuals can protect their emotional well-being and maintain personal integrity within interactions. We explored various types of physical, emotional, and time-related boundaries and highlighted how they serve as guiding principles for self-care and balanced connections. The need for clear communication was underscored as it allows partners to understand each other's boundaries without feeling threatened or dismissed.

Furthermore, the chapter focused on resolving boundary violations constructively by advocating for open dialogue and mutual understanding. Employing "I statements" was recommended to express emotions and concerns calmly, fostering an environment conducive to collaborative solutions. We also stressed the significance of forgiveness and actionable change in rebuilding trust after breaches occur. Through ongoing reflection and intentional practice, couples can adapt to evolving needs and sustain healthy boundaries that nurture more profound, meaningful relationships.

Chapter 13
Encouraging Self-Awareness

ENCOURAGING SELF-AWARENESS is pivotal for nurturing healthier relationships. When individuals look inward and engage with their inner emotions, they initiate a journey toward more profound understanding, not just of themselves but those around them. This exploration is more than an abstract pursuit; it's a practical approach to building resilient and genuine connections. It involves recognizing how past experiences shape present reactions and learning to understand these influences in a way that empowers rather than confines. As self-awareness deepens, it lays the groundwork for a relational dynamic emphasizing empathy, respect, and mutual growth.

This chapter delves into the intricacies of introspection and its role in fostering meaningful interactions. We begin by exploring the concept of personal triggers—those moments where seemingly innocuous situations provoke strong emotional responses—and how understanding these can mitigate conflicts. Moreover, the chapter guides readers through developing strategies for managing these triggers effectively, drawing from mindfulness practices and other coping techniques to maintain emotional balance. Communicating openly about one's emotional landscape becomes crucial, allowing partners to engage in constructive dialogues rather than confrontational exchanges. Finally, we examine how shared vulnerability in discussing these triggers can strengthen relationships by promoting trust and compassion, paving the way for lasting connections. Through these discussions, the chapter offers readers insights into cultivating a richer self-awareness, ultimately leading to more profound and satisfying relationships.

Identifying and Managing Personal Triggers

Understanding and identifying emotional triggers is crucial in minimizing conflicts within relationships. Emotional triggers are specific situations, behaviors, or words that provoke strong emotional reactions. Recognizing these can significantly clarify personal sensitivities, allowing individuals to navigate their relationships more smoothly and reduce misunderstandings.

One key reason these triggers form is due to past experiences, often rooted in childhood. Our current emotional responses stem from deep-seated memories or experiences during our formative years. For example, if someone grew up feeling neglected, they might react strongly to perceived indifference in their adult relationships. By acknowledging how these childhood experiences influence present-day triggers, individuals gain valuable context for their reactions, which is the first step toward gaining control over them.

Communicating these triggers clearly with loved ones can transform relationships and prevent disagreements. When partners understand each other's triggers, they are better equipped to engage in empathetic dialogues rather than arguing over misunderstandings. Consider a situation where one partner strongly reacts to raised voices because it reminds them of their parent's arguments. If this trigger is communicated effectively, the other partner can adjust their approach, perhaps by lowering their tone during disagreements, fostering a safer environment for constructive dialogue.

Developing coping strategies is another essential component of managing emotional triggers effectively. These strategies serve as a buffer, helping individuals handle triggering situations without succumbing to instantaneous emotional upheaval. One such approach involves breathing deeply and grounding oneself when a trigger arises. When emotions run high, stepping back from the situation and focusing on physical sensations can bring immediate relief, preventing rash actions or words.

Moreover, coping strategies contribute to long-term emotional resilience. Engaging in mindfulness practices, such as meditation or yoga, enhances one's ability to remain calm under pressure. Regular practice can increase awareness of emotional states, providing tools to process feelings constructively. As research suggests, mindfulness can aid in regulating emotions and reducing the intensity of emotional responses over time (<i>My Partner Triggers My Trauma: Tips and Coping Strategies</i>, 2023).

Creating a trigger management plan is another proactive step readers can take toward fostering healthier relationships. This plan could include predetermined phrases or signals to communicate the need for a pause during heated moments. For example, an agreed-upon phrase like "I need a moment to breathe" creates a mutually understood signal for temporary space, allowing both parties to regroup and return to the conversation with clearer minds. Having a plan in place not only provides structure but also alleviates the anxiety associated with potential conflict.

Furthermore, sharing and discussing emotional triggers can encourage vulnerability and strengthen emotional connections. Partners who actively listen to each other's concerns demonstrate care and commitment, reinforcing trust within the relationship. Learning about each other's triggers paves the way for shared responsibility in navigating them, ultimately leading to deeper understanding and compassion.

In addition to recognizing and communicating triggers, reflecting on behavior patterns is beneficial. By examining how frequently specific triggers occur and the circumstances surrounding them, individuals can uncover underlying causes that may need addressing. For instance, repeated conflicts over similar issues might indicate unresolved emotional needs or desires within the relationship. Addressing these root causes promotes healing and fosters a more harmonious partnership.

Validation plays a pivotal role in managing emotional triggers. When individuals feel heard and their emotions acknowledged, it can diffuse tension and foster meaningful conversations. Statements like "I see why you felt upset when that happened" convey empathy and understanding, turning potentially charged interactions into opportunities for connection. In contrast, dismissive responses may exacerbate triggers and lead to defensive or aggressive reactions.

Recognizing Patterns and Fostering Intuition

Recognizing recurring behaviors within ourselves and our relationships is a decisive step toward intentional change. Reflecting on how we interact and react over time can bring to light emotional habits that may not serve us well. It's like holding up a mirror, offering a chance for accountability and growth in our interactions. This reflection helps identify patterns that might have seemed inconsequential but are pivotal in shaping the health of our relationships.

Consider the nature of your interactions—are there repetitive reactions or emotions that crop up in various scenarios? These patterns might be indicative of more profound emotional echoes. Tracing back these behaviors can reveal much about our subconscious influences and how they guide our responses. Accountability plays a crucial role here; acknowledging these patterns allows for transformation. It's about taking ownership of actions and recognizing their impact, not only on ourselves but also on those around us.

Reflective practices can serve as a foundation for this examination. Documenting experiences and choices made through intuition is another layer that enriches self-awareness. We create a roadmap of our inner guidance system when we record our intuitive decisions. This process fosters confidence, aligning decision-making with true desires rather than external pressures or fleeting impulses. Over time, seeing the outcomes of these intuitive choices builds trust in oneself and enhances the ability to navigate life's complexities with assurance.

In addition to written reflections, creative expression can illuminate consistent themes and responses within us. Artistic endeavors—writing, painting, or music—provide a canvas to explore emotions and thoughts abstractly, often revealing insights hidden beneath the surface. This form of expression aids in cultivating emotional awareness, allowing us to see a broader picture of our internal landscape.

Continual self-assessment is vital to preventing stagnant thinking. Humans tend to gravitate towards comfort zones, which can lead to entrenched biases. Regular introspection helps identify these biases and ensures we remain open and adaptable. Mindfulness practices are particularly effective, promoting presence and reflection about emotions as they arise. By intentionally observing our thoughts and feelings without judgment, we gain clarity and can adjust our perspectives accordingly.

Seeking feedback from trusted friends or partners can further solidify our understanding of our behavioral patterns. Encouraging open conversations about mutual observations fosters a supportive environment where growth is possible. Others may notice aspects of our behavior that we might overlook, providing valuable external perspectives that challenge our internal narratives.

Bias acknowledgment is another critical component. Identifying personal biases requires honesty and willingness to examine uncomfortable truths. It's about understanding how preconceived notions influence our perceptions and interactions. Embracing this practice paves the way for adaptive strategies that propel personal and relational development.

An essential part of working with biases involves actively seeking diverse viewpoints and embracing intellectual humility. This means owning up to moments when we've been wrong and cultivating curiosity to delve deeper into other perspectives. Such openness facilitates richer dialogues and creates space for meaningful change within ourselves and our relationships.

Final Insights

Reflecting on the ideas presented in this chapter, it becomes evident that introspection is pivotal in fostering healthier relationships. Individuals can navigate emotional responses more thoughtfully by identifying personal triggers and understanding their origins. Recognizing how past experiences shape present interactions allows for greater control over reactions, minimizing conflicts with loved ones. Effective communication about these triggers paves the way for deeper connections as partners learn to engage empathetically and work collaboratively toward resolving misunderstandings. Through this process, we emphasize the importance of vulnerability and mutual understanding in strengthening bonds with others.

Moving beyond identification and communication, the chapter highlights the significance of developing coping strategies and examining behavioral patterns. Establishing a trigger management plan encourages proactive handling of potential conflicts, offering clarity and structure in tension. Engaging in reflective practices deepens one's insight into recurring emotions, prompting accountability and growth within relationships. The chapter advocates for continuous self-assessment and openness to external feedback, nurturing an environment conducive to personal and relational development. Introspection and a commitment to adapting and embracing diverse perspectives ultimately lead to more meaningful and satisfying connections.

Chapter 14
Embracing Uncertainty

EMBRACING UNCERTAINTY is an integral part of navigating the unpredictable aspects of relationships. Constant changes mark life's journey, and nowhere is this more evident than within our connections with others. Relationships evolve; they face challenges and transitions that can be daunting and enlightening. Each shift allows us to understand our partners or friends and ourselves better. By exploring uncertainty from different perspectives, we gain insights into how these changes can foster growth and deepen understanding. In this acceptance of unpredictability, we find room for personal and relational development.

In this chapter, readers will explore various strategies to adapt to changes gracefully and accept the unpredictable nature of human connections. The discussion includes methods to enhance communication skills, ensuring that transitions are transparent and open. Through anecdotes and practical advice, the chapter delves into how proactive communication acts as a tool to maintain harmony and build trust. Additionally, it touches on the importance of learning new coping mechanisms and seeking mentorship, showcasing how support systems can empower us during times of change. Techniques like mindfulness and resilience-building exercises are presented as ways to manage anxiety associated with uncertainty. The chapter concludes with insights into creating supportive networks, emphasizing the role of community and shared experiences in overcoming relational unpredictability.

Adapting to Change Gracefully and Accepting Unpredictability

Embracing transitions in relationships is a pivotal aspect of understanding the broader journey of life. It's essential to acknowledge that change is inevitable and a crucial part of our relational dynamics. Recognizing change as natural can alleviate the fear often accompanying it, transforming challenges into opportunities. This outlook encourages us to embrace shifts within relationships with an open mind and a willingness to adapt.

Proactive communication is one of the most effective tools in navigating these transitions. In any familial, romantic, or platonic relationship, the ability to express thoughts and feelings openly can prevent misunderstandings and foster a deeper connection. Engaging in regular conversations about future goals, expectations, and even fears can create a foundation of trust and mutual understanding. For instance, when a couple discusses their evolving roles or aspirations, they are more likely to support each other through changes rather than resist them.

Learning new coping strategies can significantly aid in adjusting to transitions. Life is replete with countless instances where we must adapt—moving to a new city, starting a new job, or dealing with the end of a relationship. We can gain valuable insights and practical advice by actively seeking mentorship or guidance from those who have navigated similar experiences. Sometimes, hearing someone else's journey to feel empowered is all it takes. Moreover, mentorship isn't confined to formal settings. It could be a conversation with a trusted friend or family member who provides invaluable perspective.

Reframing uncertainty requires consciously shifting from a fear-based approach to a growth-oriented one. Viewing uncertainty as an opportunity for connection and personal development helps dismantle the walls that fear builds around us. For example, entering a new phase in a relationship, like deciding to live together or becoming parents, might initially seem daunting. However, by perceiving these events as chances to grow together and learn more about one another, couples can enhance their bond significantly.

Mindfulness practices offer a pathway to handle the anxiety that unpredictability may bring. Mindfulness encourages being present in the moment, acknowledging feelings without judgment, and fostering a sense of calmness even amidst chaos. Simple techniques like deep breathing exercises, meditation, or mindful listening during conversations can ground individuals and provide clarity. These practices promote emotional regulation, which is critical in maintaining composure and resilience when faced with unexpected changes.

Building resilience entails cultivating skills that bolster one's capacity to withstand life's fluctuations. Resilience doesn't mean avoiding stress; it's about strengthening your ability to recover from setbacks. Developing habits such as gratitude journaling or reflecting on past experiences where you've successfully managed change can reinforce this mindset. You might remember a time when a sudden career shift led you to a much more fulfilling path, thereby reminding yourself of the potential of the positive outcome in uncertainty.

To effectively manage transitions, creating a supportive network is imperative. A robust support system can significantly affect how we cope with change. Encouraging readers to cultivate relationships with friends, family, and peers adds layers of support and provides diverse perspectives, enhancing our understanding of varied situations. Additionally, joining groups or communities that resonate with one's experiences, whether online or in real life, offers a space to share stories and gather strength from collective wisdom.

Managing Insecurities Positively and Seeing Uncertainty as an Opportunity

In any relationship, confronting personal insecurities can be daunting yet rewarding. These insecurities often stem from deep-seated feelings of inadequacy, which might have roots in past experiences or low self-esteem (LMHC, 2022). Enhancing self-awareness is the first crucial step toward understanding and improving relational dynamics. By identifying these personal insecurities, individuals can begin recognizing patterns of doubt or fear that affect their interactions. Journaling or reflective discussions with a partner can aid in uncovering these hidden aspects of oneself, allowing for more honest communication.

Transforming insecurities into growth opportunities requires deliberate and actionable steps. Consider starting with small changes by setting realistic expectations within your relationship. For instance, when jealousy arises, instead of succumbing to negative thoughts, view these moments as chances to engage in meaningful dialogue with your partner. Sharing these vulnerabilities can deepen the emotional connection and promote mutual understanding. Open communication is critical; partners should regularly discuss their needs and fears in a safe space without fear of judgment. This practice builds trust and encourages both individuals to support each other's growth journey.

Uncertainty within relationships, while often feared, can catalyze innovation and positive change. Reflecting on past instances where unpredictability led to unexpected joy or learning can help reframe one's perspective on uncertainty. Such an approach fosters resilience and adaptability, qualities essential for thriving relationships. Encouraging a mindset that embraces this ambiguity allows couples to venture out of their comfort zones and explore new ways of relating to each other.

One practical guideline for navigating uncertain scenarios together is to establish shared goals and experiences. Planning joint activities or setting common objectives can create a sense of unity and purpose, even amidst unpredictability. Whether it's learning a new skill together or tackling a challenge as a team, these experiences can strengthen the bond between partners and open up new avenues for exploration. Engaging in open dialogues about future aspirations and dreams—individual and collective—can pave the way for deeper understanding and collaboration.

Building a supportive environment is essential in cultivating a robust relationship. It involves creating a safe space where individuals feel comfortable expressing themselves freely. Establishing routines reinforcing security, like regular check-ins or designated times for discussing concerns, can enhance this supportive atmosphere. Additionally, cultivating emotional anchors or practices that ground the relationship during turbulent times, such as shared rituals or affirmations, can provide stability.

In the context of exploring new avenues together, it is crucial to remember the importance of risk and reward. Venturing into unknown territory can be intimidating, but it holds immense growth and fulfillment potential. Knowing that risks are taken with a partner who supports and uplifts you makes the uncertainty more manageable and less daunting. Together, couples can navigate these waters, turning potential threats into opportunities for more robust connections and a richer shared experience.

Concluding Thoughts

As we navigate the unpredictable aspects of relationships, we must recognize that these shifts are not merely obstacles but avenues for growth and understanding. The unpredictability of relationships can test us, yet it also presents unique opportunities to deepen our connections and expand our horizons. By embracing these changes with an open heart and a mindset willing to adapt, we can transform uncertainty into a powerful tool for building stronger bonds. Through proactive communication and developing new coping strategies, individuals can learn to see challenges as shared experiences that bring partners closer.

Reflecting on our personal and shared experiences helps us manage insecurities positively and view uncertainty as an opportunity rather than a threat. When couples engage in meaningful dialogues about their goals, fears, and aspirations, they build a foundation of trust that supports individual and mutual growth. Creating a supportive environment makes partners feel secure enough to take risks together, fostering resilience and adaptability. In this dynamic give-and-take, each step into the unknown promises deeper connection and enriched shared journeys. Ultimately, these ever-evolving dynamics enhance the present relationship and provide lasting insights for future partnerships.

Chapter 15
The Journey to Authentic Connection

FORMING AUTHENTIC CONNECTIONS is a journey filled with opportunities for growth and discovery. As individuals seek to establish meaningful relationships, it becomes essential to acknowledge the value of consistent efforts and openness in fostering these bonds. Building such connections requires more than just fleeting interactions; it involves a long-term commitment to understanding diverse perspectives and prioritizing quality engagement. Authentic connections don't just happen overnight—they are cultivated through intentional actions and an ongoing dedication to relationship work. Readers will find that this chapter provides insightful guidance on navigating this intricate yet rewarding path.

In this chapter, readers will explore various steps to achieve consistent and meaningful interactions that form the basis of authentic connections. Covering aspects such as setting clear intentions and actively engaging with others, the text delves into how these practices create a foundation of trust and authenticity in relationships. It emphasizes embracing vulnerability and revisiting meaningful conversations over time, illuminating how these elements help nurture deeper bonds. Through practical advice and examples, readers will gain insights into making every interaction significant and ensuring that each connection grows more robust and resilient over time. The focus remains on creating relationships where both parties feel understood and appreciated, reflecting a commitment to ongoing personal and relational development.

Steps to Achieving Consistent and Meaningful Interactions

To cultivate authentic connections, starting with clear intentions is paramount. Intentions are the foundation of any relationship, paving the way for trust and authenticity. When you communicate your purpose effectively, it establishes a sense of security in the other party, ensuring that your actions align with your commitments. For instance, if you're meeting someone new, whether it's in a personal or professional context, expressing your genuine interest in understanding their perspective can set a positive tone for future interactions. You lay the groundwork for a relationship built on trust by openly stating your desire for a meaningful connection. Active engagement is another essential component in fostering deeper connections. Active participation goes beyond merely being present; it involves being genuinely involved in conversations and activities. It shows respect for the other person's thoughts and feelings, demonstrating a sincere desire to connect. This might mean actively listening when someone speaks, asking thoughtful questions, or remembering details from past conversations. Such gestures convey attentiveness and care, strengthening the relational bond. Imagine how much more valued someone feels when they realize you are invested in what they have to share. This dedication enriches the immediate interaction and fortifies the long-term connection by making each encounter significant.

Embracing vulnerability plays a critical role in creating profound and trusting relationships. Opening up and sharing personal experiences or feelings fosters an environment where both parties feel comfortable being themselves. Vulnerability facilitates closeness by allowing others to see beyond surface appearances and understand someone's genuine self. Sharing struggles or admitting uncertainties can be daunting, yet these acts often lead to profound understanding and mutual respect. When you take the brave step to be vulnerable, it usually encourages others to reciprocate, resulting in deeper layers of trust and empathy. For example, discussing personal challenges with a friend can lead to more supportive and understanding dynamics in the relationship, as each person sees the other's authentic self without the filters of pretense.

As relationships evolve, revisiting meaningful conversations over time is a powerful practice for nurturing bonds. Regularly touching base on significant discussions or unresolved matters shows that you value the relationship enough to ensure ongoing growth and clarity. Revisiting past dialogues demonstrates a commitment to resolving issues and celebrating progress, keeping the relationship dynamic and adaptable to change. These follow-up interactions strengthen relational ties by reinforcing shared goals and understanding. They highlight the journey undertaken together and allow space for reflection and adaptation. Whether checking in with a partner about previous agreements or discussing evolving views on a topic with a friend, it signifies dedication to maintaining and enhancing the connection (Perez, 2023).

This cycle of revisiting and reflecting provides opportunities for both individuals to express their growth and evolving needs. It signifies that the relationship is valued and worth investing effort into. Moreover, it underscores a willingness to adapt and grow alongside one another, which is crucial for sustained connection. Setting a guideline here—perhaps scheduling regular times to revisit topics—can ensure that critical conversations remain active parts of your relational dialogue. These actionable steps collectively reinforce practices that lead to deep, authentic connections. Establishing intentions, engaging actively, embracing vulnerability, and revisiting critical conversations are not just isolated activities but interconnected facets of building meaningful interactions. Each step nurtures an aspect of the relationship, contributing to a stronger, more resilient bond overall.

Practical implementation of these concepts can start small, such as setting aside time to reflect on your intentions before essential interactions. Practice active listening during everyday conversations by focusing entirely on the speaker and responding thoughtfully. Encourage a culture of openness by sharing your personal story and inviting others to do the same. Make it a habit to revisit past discussions periodically, checking how perspectives might have changed over time. These efforts create an atmosphere ripe for genuine connection, allowing relationships to thrive in authenticity and depth.

Commitment and Openness for Long-term Relationship Growth

Forming deep, meaningful connections requires a consistent and determined approach, as it is a journey that necessitates ongoing dedication. Cultivating these relationships is about building trust, understanding, and valuing each other through constant interaction. Regular communication is the foundation of this effort, as the bridge that connects partners over time.

Communication is not just about talking; it's about effectively conveying thoughts, emotions, and intentions to foster a sense of trust. When partners engage in open and regular dialogue, they create an atmosphere where both feel understood and appreciated. This steady exchange helps to cultivate mutual respect and reliability, making each person feel valued. By adopting active listening skills and empathic responses, individuals reinforce their commitment to each other, showing that they genuinely care about what the other is experiencing (PSYLANCER Administrator, 2023).

Beyond regular dialogue, having transparent intentions and holding oneself accountable is crucial for fostering trust. Transparency means being honest and transparent about one's motives and desires within the relationship. It involves sharing thoughts without hidden agendas, which reassures partners of each other's sincerity. Similarly, accountability ensures that one's actions are aligned with their words. When partners assume responsibility for their actions, they demonstrate reliability, further deepening trust. These elements combine to fortify a connection, ensuring both parties feel secure and supported.

Another significant aspect of nurturing relationships involves celebrating shared milestones and embracing diverse perspectives. Recognizing and cherishing personal or collective achievements creates a sense of joy and accomplishment within the partnership. This celebration reinforces positivity and strengthens bonds, fostering an environment where happiness can thrive (PSYLANCER Administrator, 2023). Acknowledging diversity in thoughts and backgrounds enriches the relationship by promoting empathy and understanding. Each partner brings unique experiences and viewpoints, and when these are embraced, it fosters a collaborative spirit that enhances relational depth. Diverse perspectives can offer fresh insights and solutions, broadening the relational horizon and encouraging adaptive growth. Couples who engage in continuous personal development and adapt their communication strategies are often more satisfied in their relationships. Personal growth allows partners to continually bring a better version of themselves into the relationship. Each person can contribute positively to the dynamic by focusing on individual pursuits and development. Meanwhile, adapting communication strategies to suit changing circumstances ensures that discussions remain productive and supportive. This adaptability reflects a willingness to evolve alongside the relationship, accommodating new challenges and changes as they arise. The investment of consistent efforts in relationships mirrors the broader investment in life itself—requiring patience, perseverance, and a genuine interest in nurturing growth. Just as gardeners tend to a plant, attending to its needs while allowing it space to thrive, so must partners approach their relationship with diligence and respect for each other's individuality. This metaphor underscores the delicate balance between care and freedom, highlighting the importance of nurturing without stifling.

Summary and Reflections

This chapter explored the essential elements needed for forming deep and meaningful connections. We discussed how setting clear intentions can lay a strong foundation for trust and authenticity in relationships. By practicing active engagement, like listening carefully and showing genuine interest, we can make others feel valued and respected. Embracing vulnerability is also crucial; opening up and sharing personal experiences allows for a more profound understanding and empathy between individuals. Revisiting meaningful conversations ensures relationships remain dynamic and adaptable to change, providing opportunities to address unresolved issues and celebrate progress. Looking ahead, it's clear that relationships thrive on consistency and openness. Regular communication acts as the lifeline connecting partners, fostering a sense of trust and mutual respect. Being transparent and accountable reinforces our commitment to the relationship, making each partner feel secure. Celebrating shared milestones and embracing diverse perspectives further enriches the connection, adding layers of depth and understanding. Cultivating satisfying connections requires patience and dedication, like tending to a growing plant. Investing time and effort while respecting individuality creates an environment where relationships can flourish authentically and robustly.

to reconsider their approaches to competition, ambition, and life's uncertain journey.

** About the Author **

Willy Lapse Laguerre is a writer and thinker with a deep fascination for the human psyche and the mysteries of life's challenges. With a background in psychology and philosophy, Laguerre's work delves into the complex interplay between ambition, resilience, and the subtle yet profound forces that drive human behavior. His writing is known for its thought-provoking exploration of themes like self-discovery, inner conflict, and the emotional struggles that arise in a world full of unspoken expectations.

Laguerre's journey as an author has been shaped by his own experiences of confronting life's "unwinnable games"—the persistent inner battles that, rather than ending in victory or defeat, transform us in unexpected ways. He is dedicated to shedding light on the nuances of the human condition and inspiring readers to find purpose and meaning in both their victories and their losses.

When not writing, Laguerre can be found hiking through nature, searching for fresh perspectives, or immersed in conversations with those who share his passion for understanding life's deeper questions. "The Game You Can Never Win" marks a significant contribution to his growing body of work, offering readers a unique lens through which to view life's ongoing challenges.

Don't miss out!

Visit the website below and you can sign up to receive emails whenever Willy Lapse Laguerre publishes a new book. There's no charge and no obligation.

https://books2read.com/r/B-A-QNFNC-TFUHF

BOOKS 2 READ

Connecting independent readers to independent writers.

Did you love *The Game You Can Never Win*? Then you should read *The Forbidden Love*[1] by Willy Lapse Laguerre!

The Secret Garden

In the heart of a bustling city, nestled between tall buildings and busy streets, there lay a secret garden known only to a few. It was a place of tranquility, a sanctuary where time seemed to slow down. This hidden gem played a significant role in the love story of Emma, a talented artist with a fiery spirit, and Alexander, a dedicated doctor bound by family expectations. Emma had accidentally discovered the garden one summer day while sketching in the park. Intrigued by the hidden entrance covered in ivy, she pushed through and found herself in a world of blooming flowers and the soft hum of nature. She had been coming back ever since, using the serene environment to inspire

---

1. https://books2read.com/u/mVPw1M

2. https://books2read.com/u/mVPw1M

her art. Alexander stumbled upon the garden during a particularly stressful week at the hospital. Seeking peace, he wandered through the city until he found the secluded spot. From the moment he entered, he knew it would become his refuge. Their paths crossed one evening as the sun dipped below the horizon, casting a golden hue over the garden. Emma was perched on a stone bench, her sketchpad balanced on her knee, while Alexander stood by a rose bush, inhaling the sweet scent of the flowers. Their eyes met, and in that instant, a connection was forged. Over the following months, Emma and Alexander met regularly in the garden. They shared their dreams and fears, their laughter and sorrows." Emma spoke of her desire to break free from the constraints of society and pursue her art without limits. Alexander confided in her about the pressures of his family, who expected him to follow in his father's footsteps and marry a woman of their choosing. Their bond grew stronger with each passing day, and soon, it blossomed into love. But it was a love shrouded in secrecy. Alexander's Emma, Ifather's family would never approve of Emma, a free-spirited artist without regard for social status. And Emma, fiercely independent, feared losing herself to the expectations of Alexander's world. Alexander took Emma's hand as they sought shelter under a large oak tree one rainy evening. "Emma'sI can't keep living this lie," he said, his voice heavy with emotion. "I love you, Emma. I want to be with you, no matter what." Emma's heart ached at his words. She wanted to be with him, too, more than anything. But the reality of their situation loomed over them. "Alex, your family will never accept us. They'll force you to choose between them and me."